BROTHERHOOD: THE SECOND CHAPTER

A NOVEL BY: RAHUL MINHAS

About the Book

"Brotherhood: The Second Chapter" is an immersive and compelling fiction novel crafted to resonate with young readers while equally captivating adults. By delving into the themes of bullying, the underlying fear of becoming a victim, and the internal struggle for acceptance within the younger generation, this book skillfully navigates the intricate landscape of human emotions. More specifically, the book goes beyond surface-level examination and delves into the lasting impact of bullying trauma, highlighting how it leads the main-character, Manav, to engage in at-risk behaviors and unhealthy attachments. As the pages turn, readers witness the remarkable evolution of the main character from the vulnerable stages of youth to the confident realm of adulthood.

Dedication

To my pet dog, Apollo. You have brought immeasurable joy to my life, and I am grateful for every moment we have spent together. You have been a constant source of happiness and inspiration, and I dedicate this book to you.

Chapter One

"We have live updates and video footage detailing the war between Ukraine and Russia," the anchorman says. "Soldiers are moving with vicious intent and minimal chances of a peaceful resolution in the near future."

"Imagine the unimaginable," Manav says in response to the news coverage.

Shelby tilts her head away from her computer screen and looks at Manav. "What are you referring to, Manav? What's unimaginable?"

"You have stability in your life until one day you wake up, take a deep stretch and open your blinds, and you witness a war in your own backyard," Manav replies.

Shelby nods, walks to the back corner of the office, and turns off the staticky, dark gray television. "A different perspective, but reasonable. It is an alarming event, but it is happening in a different part of the world." She redirects the conversation by adding, "Concentrating on improving your health, graduating on time, and excelling in soccer and basketball should be your primary focuses." She slowly walks back to her office chair after shutting off the television.

Maraino, Manav's community therapist, opens his office door, takes a small step out and looks at Manav with a smile. "Manav! It has been a long time since I last saw you here. Feel free to come into my office now so we can work through your thoughts and feelings regarding today's incident."

Manav stands tall from his chair with his head held high, then he takes a slow, deep breath that reaches the bottom of his stomach to help him relax. He enters his doors slowly while mentally preparing himself for what he believes will be Maraino's irrelevant, uninteresting lecture about using positive coping skills whenever he feels upset or angry.

"Today might be a great day to make the most of this session," Shelby whispers to Manav as he enters Maraino's office.

"Feel free to grab that chair right there," Maraino tells him. "Now, Manav, with our sessions, you can feel free to express your thoughts and feelings, but I need you to do your best to be truthful right now. I need you to do your best to be transparent. How would you evaluate these past few months for yourself?"

Confidently, Manav replies, "I would say I have accomplished many goals these past few months. My basketball team has four wins and zero losses, and my soccer team continues to compete in the playoffs. I've succeeded a lot this year."

Maraino gives Manav an awkward smile, then stares at him with a firm look. "That is an excellent assessment of your participation in sports this year. However, about your behaviours, what are your thoughts about that?"

"Well, why don't you explain?" Manav asks him.

Maraino turns around and analyzes Manav's file in front of him and says, "According to the notes from your parents and your other support workers, you were strong academically and demonstrated good behaviour while, of course, participating in sports and other community programs, in grades eight, nine, and ten. However, your grade eleven year has shown many overall changes. Your dad mentions that you are on the verge of needing to repeat math, you miss the first class of school too often to sleep in, and today was the fourth fight you have been involved in this year. He also mentioned that you act a bit angrily with them at home, which they have not seen previously."

"Maraino, Marcus is a malicious bully," Manav interrupts, "and I've spoken to you about him before during our sessions together. He always takes things from my locker and shoves me in the hallways to show his toughness. Everyone has a breaking point, and he crossed that line today, so I had to let him know about it."

Maraino turns around from viewing Manav's file on his desk and begins empathizing with his perspective. "I recall you sharing some of your feelings about him in our previous sessions, Manav. You feel Marcus's attitude towards you has been tough for you to handle, and you feel some aggression towards it. Do you feel it was reasonable to fight him back?"

Manav stands from his chair and says to him in a firm voice, "The only thing I regret is that every kid has a phone. Every kid has a camera attached to that phone, and from the clips I saw, I know those images could be out in the public forever. Aside from this, it would be best if you saw that my actions were reasonable.

3

Does your mind ever become blank from having built-up anger?"

"It looks like you are getting elevated, so please have a seat," Maraino suggests.

Manav sits back in his chair and uses his hand to massage the side of his head as he feels a headache from Maraino's comments. "It looks like we are done here," he tells Maraino. "I have also been told that I have to step away from school for a few days to get my mind together, so maybe I will see you next week."

Manav and Maraino share a brief pause, then Maraino stares out of his blinds and sees a group of kids walking past his window. He says to Manav, "I met you when you were thirteen years of age, Manav. I was intrigued that your family had concerns about you and that you were seeking help from a therapist. From the average eye, some would say you are as complete a person as you could be, but I always say you never know what someone is going through in their day. Manav, do you remember what you said to me when we first met?"

"We do not need to talk about that day," Manav replies as he chuckles. "I was just a kid at the time when I felt that, and I am not sure if that feeling is relevant to what's happening today."

Manav reaches for his bag to take out his headphones and cellphone to listen to music on his walk home. He recognizes it is at the bottom of his backpack under his soccer gear and textbook, so he takes out all these items to grab them. As he reaches for his music player, the necklace in his bag gets caught in the cord of his earphones and fumbles to the ground.

Maraino glances at it and comments, "Has that necklace always been yours? That is a unique shape at the front of it."

Manav picks up the chain from the floor and shows Maraino as it hangs from his palm. "This belonged to my dad's eldest brother, who lived with us for a few years. He wore it as a kid while working on his farm, which is well-known today. The farm is about eighty years old, but he expanded it about forty years ago to create more work opportunities for people in the community. Also, he provides housing for most of his employees by letting them live in his large house next to the farm."

Maraino takes the chain from Manav's palm. "I remember speaking to your dad about this over the summer. He said your uncle supported you while living with you, too, before he passed on."

Manav nods in response, stands from his chair and is ready to leave Maraino's clinic. Before he does, Maraino points at Manav's textbook, which is still lying on the floor. "Don't forget to take that with you. It will collect dust if you do not work away at it."

Manav grabs his textbook from the ground, takes a brief look at it, and replies, "I do not have time to learn algebra," then tosses it on Maraino's desk and walks out of his office.

Maraino takes the textbook from his desk, power-walks behind Manav, and unzips his backpack. "Here, I will help you pack it in your bag for you."

They walk to the front of the clinic, where Manav puts his hand in a fist to give Maraino a fist bump goodbye. Instead, with a smile, Mariano sticks his hand flat out to give Manav a handshake. "I am fifty-four years old, so I am unfamiliar with a fist bump. A simple handshake works fine for me."

Maraino and Manav exchange a handshake, and he proceeds to go home.

After taking a few steps out of his office, Manav stops in his tracks as he sees an older youth across the street staring at him.

He is roughly six foot three, with a thin but muscular build and a blue tattoo on his upper arm that looks like it was done in prison. Manav takes a closer look and recognizes that it's Noah, a relative of Marcus, but he isn't sure exactly how they are specifically related. He notices that Noah is giving him a firm, angry look, as he is likely upset that he had trouble with Marcus today. Manav pauses to make brief eye contact with him, then continues his trip home.

After walking for approximately ten minutes, Manav looks back and notices that Noah continues to stare at him from a distance. "An ugly choice for a tattoo," Manav mutters to himself. "That's what you should worry about."

Manav finally reaches home after a twenty-minute walk from Maraino's office. He is a few steps away from the front entrance of his home, but before he can open the door, his mother, in pyjamas and wielding a wooden spatula, swings open the door. She quickly looks at Manav and then returns to the kitchen to resume cooking. He assumes she is being dismissive because she heard about his altercation at school. However, Cooper, Manav's pet dog, dashes out the door and jumps at Manav with all four legs.

"You can take notes on how nice Cooper is to me," Manav tells her.

He enters his home and places his backpack next to the bottom of the stairs, then he raises his arms roughly halfway in the air and says to his mom, "You want to lecture me first?"

Manav's mom moves her head left to right a few times. "Your dad is making shipments in another province. I will let him take charge of this situation once he's back, and I am sure he will be excited to speak to you."

Manav puts his arms down and knows this issue is serious

since she has not explicitly addressed today's incident. He turns around, grabs his bag, and heads upstairs. After reaching the third step, he pauses, walks back down, and tries to ease his mom's intense energy by complimenting her. "The food you are putting together smells like another classic."

Manav's mom does not acknowledge his comments and continues to look straight ahead at the stovetop.

Manav decides to nag her a bit more. "You can turn it into a business, and maybe we will become business partners and pay off this mortgage, or sell this dump and get a larger home."

She breaks from her intense posture and energy and starts laughing. "I will pass on being business partners with you," she replies. "If we had to deal with angry customers, you might lack self-control as you did with Marcus today."

"That is an impressive response, but you know only I make the jokes around here, Mom, so where did you learn a comeback like that?" Manav teases.

"I have been spending a little too much time around you," she tells him.

After a short discussion with his mom, he grabs his backpack and goes upstairs to his bedroom. He lays on his bed with his hands behind his head and stares at the ceiling, then he glances at Cooper and says, "At least we got a few days off, Coop..." *(Buzz Buzz).*

Manav's phone begins to vibrate on top of his desk, so he reaches over to check the number and recognizes it is his dad attempting to video call him. He contemplates answering his call, but before the end of the fourth ring, he decides to answer.

"Manav, can you hear me?" are the first words his dad shouts.

"Hello, Hello, Dad. I hear you loud and clear, but I have to say, the long working hours on the road are starting to make you look a little rough," Manav says in greeting.

"Manav, you think this is a game? Well, this is not a game," his dad replies in an angry tone. "I work ten-hour shifts, seven days a week, so I can give you what you ask. Do you think this is an acceptable way to live your life?"

"If life were a game, Dad, to be honest, I would be incredible at it. I strive with games, especially when playing online on my PlayStation," Manav replies sarcastically.

"Manav, be serious," he tells him. "What will happen if you end up with a criminal record for fighting? Have you thought of that? You may as well get a job now flipping burgers and giving people fries if you are going to get in trouble and not complete school."

"If I served people fries, burgers, and pop all day, at least I would have some good food to bring home at the end of every night," Manav says, continuing to use sarcastic language with his dad.

"But that is not how you will get ahead," his dad replies. The screen becomes dark as Manav's dad ends the call with him.

Chapter Two

"What's with the noise out there?" Manav murmurs as he gets out of bed.

      Manav goes to bed after speaking to his dad over a video call. That night, he twists and turns in bed from having trouble falling asleep and periodically wakes up throughout the night. Roughly a quarter after five in the morning, he slowly opens his eyes and notices red and blue lights circulating in his bedroom. Cooper is growling at the curtains as if a dangerous situation is occurring outside. Manav removes his blanket and decides to walk over to the blinds and lifts it slightly enough to take a small peek.

      As he looks outside, he notices three police officers entering a home located down the block, and they leave the house after several minutes with his neighbour in handcuffs. Manav is amazed at how his neighbour shows little emotion as he is arrested and escorted by the officers.

As he continues to observe this scene, his mom, who is up early working in the kitchen, shouts, "Manav, I know you are awake, so come and eat eggs and toast for breakfast!"

Manav is not surprised that his mom is aware that he is up from bed because she has that instinct of knowing his every move, so he hurries downstairs to meet her in the kitchen.

"Mom, have you ever met the person that lives down the street in our neighbourhood?" Manav asks her. "He's just got handcuffed by the police right now."

His mom shakes her head from side to side and says, "That is VJ. He and many of his friends are always involved in crimes and have had encounters with police officers since they were young. For now, do me a favour and avoid talking with people like that."

"I get what you're saying, Mom, but you already know that I can't ruin my chances of playing basketball and soccer in the big leagues by committing crimes," he tells her. "I hope to get us a huge home with all the money I make from my contracts as an athlete. We will own all the latest appliances you can think of, and I will install a high-end home gym so Dad can finally start living a healthy lifestyle."

Manav's mom has a short laugh at his remarks. "Your dad is a good-hearted man, but he can use a treadmill and some dumbbells to help himself get in better shape."

They have breakfast and lunch together, and they take Cooper for a walk around the neighbourhood afterwards. Although Manav has been asked to take time away from school after his altercation with Marcus, he is given permission to attend his sports practices and games. Therefore, around two in the afternoon, he grabs his backpack from his bedroom, which contains his gym clothes, shoes, and basketball, and he is prepared to attend basketball practice.

He and his mom arrive at Manav's school after a ten-minute car ride, and she says to him, "Show off those skills you have been working on during the summer at camp, and be nice towards your teammates, too, and maybe you will be able to establish a friendship with them."

"I will definitely show off the skills that I have put together, and being part of a group would not hurt. But to be honest, maybe I am starting to feel that I need to change my personality to be appreciated by others more," Manav replies. "There is a certain way some others behave, and how I act is entirely different from that culture. Have you ever been accepted for being yourself? Because I am confused by that idea."

Manav's mom places her hand on the back of his head to comfort him. "Just be yourself, Manav. Be patient. Be smart. Be you. Take your time," she encourages calmly.

Manav grabs his bag with his basketball gear and leaves his vehicle. He walks to the two large outside gym doors and clinches one of them as he is about to enter the gymnasium. But before he does, he sees Devin Gill, a friend he has known since childhood, talking to his dad in their car. Manav and Devin grew up playing sports together, and his dad has assisted Manav's family in buying their current home as he is a realtor.

Manav releases the gym door and walks to the passenger side of their car to connect with them. "Mr. Gill, I have not seen you since last basketball season. Devin, I look forward to our practice together today. How has life been for the both of you?"

"Manav, it has been ages since I last saw you. I guess time

flies quickly," Mr. Gill replies. "Devin always tells me how hard you work with your skills, and I can't wait to see that on the court this year. But he also mentioned that you had a little trouble with some boys this week at school. What happened?"

"Just had a bit of history with this kid, and I was in a mindset where I felt I had to take care of it myself," Manav replies.

"That is understandable. Some situations can be challenging, but what were you feeling at the time? It is not like you to do something like that," he tells Manav.

Manav appreciates Mr. Gill's empathetic response as he is never too high and never too low. He remains centred and uses a firm and fair approach. "I can figure this one out on my own," Manav answers, "but if I need any help, I will let you know."

Mr. Gill tells Manav, "We are always here for you. We will work together to help you through anything, right, Devin?" Devin nods at his dad in agreeing to support Manav. Mr. Gill adds, "Regarding myself, I am thriving in the real estate boom as I reached my sales targets, and all I can ask for is to make enough to support Devin and the family. But I will continue this chat with you later. Your practice begins in three minutes, so you should run inside to get warmed up."

Devin and Manav enter the gym, and Manav immediately recognizes Devin's improvements in his skills once they begin practicing. He glides as he dribbles and has perfect rotation on the ball after each jump shot. Once practice ends, they chat as they walk out the gym doors.

"I have to be upfront with you," Devin says. "Sorry I haven't been able to see you outside of school. I've been busy ensuring my grades are perfect, and I have to attend practices with my community teams, but we will reconnect during school breaks if that works?"

Manav understands that Devin is always occupied with activities as his family wants him to excel in school and sports. After their brief conversation, they exchange their goodbyes, and Manav is ready to walk home. He puts his earphones in to listen to music and has his basketball in his right hand. He notices frost building on the sidewalks as the sky is dark and gloomy, and the wind blows heavily.

It takes Manav roughly twenty-five minutes to walk from his school to his house, and after walking for approximately ten minutes, he begins to feel cold, so he kneels on one knee to take out his coat from his bag. He stands tall as he places it around his arms and body and zips it up firmly. He is set to continue his walk, but before he does, he quickly looks back from the corner of his eye and spots an individual walking behind him about thirty-five feet away wearing black joggers with a white zip-up done halfway. Manav resumes his trip home, but he pauses his music while still having his headphones in his ears so that he can hear the stranger's footsteps behind him.

He notices the stranger's footsteps grow louder as they close the distance to him. After walking on a high-traffic street for a few minutes, Manav takes a right into an alley and begins to power-walk. He hears the stranger's footsteps hitting the ground quicker and louder as they start to jog toward him. The random person then fully sprints to Manav in the alley, grabs him on his right shoulder, and spins him one hundred and eighty degrees to meet him face to face.

Manav looks closer at the stranger and shouts, "Noah!" and begins to backpedal slowly.

"It's time for payback for what happened to Marcus," Noah

growls menacingly.

Noah moves towards Manav, presses two hands on his chest, and shoves him a few feet back, then Noah reaches for the left pocket of his jacket and draws a sharp, stainless steel folding blade. "There is a price you have to pay for what you did."

Manav backs away to avoid getting hurt. Out of desperation to protect himself, he places his hand under his basketball and throws it full force at Noah. Unfortunately, he misses terribly, and the ball rolls down the end of the alley.

Then, Manav takes his backpack off his shoulder and attempts to strike Noah with it while keeping a safe distance from him. After a few swings, Manav connects with Noah's left arm, which causes him to drop his weapon. He then feels momentum, so he holds his bag with a firmer grip and strikes Noah repeatedly until he falls to the ground.

Manav tosses his backpack to the side and sprints to the end of the alley, and once he takes his first step on the main road, he hears the sound of sirens in the air. He looks to his left and recognizes it is coming from a police car speeding toward the scene. Out of fear, he turns around and sprints to the other end of the alley, but another police car arrives and parks sideways on that end, preventing him from escaping.

Noah remains on the ground while Manav stands in the middle of the alley, and a total of three police officers exit their cars to approach them from both sides.

Manav raises his hands in the air and repeatedly shouts, "I'm innocent!"

One of the three officers flashes their badge at Manav and says, "I am Constable Rodney, and I am trying to understand why this person is lying on the ground."

With sharp pain clawing through his chest from high anxiety levels, Manav replies, "I...I," but cannot complete his statement.

"Take a deep breath and remain calm," Officer Rodney says to him. "You're safe now."

Manav composes himself, and from the corner of his eye, he sees Noah slowly climbing to his feet after lying on the ground for several minutes. Manav pleads to Constable Rodney by telling him, "That's Noah. He tried to get me with that knife over there."

Constable Rodney grabs the weapon after Manav points it out. "Stay calm. We've had previous encounters with Noah, and we know that he can become aggressive with others."

Noah stands to his feet, and the officers immediately put handcuffs on him and escort him to the police car. Noah gives Manav a deathly stare as he leaves and says, "The chance to get payback is not over. Do you think this will be the last time you see me? I'll be there when you least expect it." Constable Rodney looks at Noah, then stares at Manav and tells him, "Do not worry about him and his comments. I will look after you tonight and drop you off at home to ensure you are safe."

"I will pass on that," Manav replies. "My parents would be angry if I came home with a police officer, which is an understatement."

Constable Rodney chuckles at his response. "Don't worry about that. I will explain exactly what happened this evening to your parents, and no one will be angry with you. You need to understand that this is just for your safety."

After some back-and-forth, Manav ultimately decides to get in Constable Rodney's vehicle to get a ride home. They have a smooth, peaceful trip back to his house, and Constable Rodney knocks firmly on his door to address his family about tonight's incident.

His mom answers, but to his surprise, his dad is behind her, making strong eye contact with Manav and Constable Rodney.

"Dad, you're home tonight?" Manav wonders.

Manav's dad steps to the front of the door and stares angrily at them, but Constable Rodney smiles back to ease the tension. "I hope you both are having a great evening," Constable Rodney says. "It's confusing when your child comes home with a police officer, but I promise you that Manav is not in trouble tonight. In fact, he is a confident, centred man who was able to handle a dangerous situation on his own, and you are fortunate to have such a brave son."

The conversation between Constable Rodney and Manav's parents ends quickly, and he gives them his contact information and phone numbers for additional community support.

Once Constable Rodney leaves, Manav's dad tells him, "We need to meet in the living room to talk."

Manav moves to this area and sits on one couch with Cooper beside him, and his parents sit on a separate sofa. His dad asks, "Why have you been involved in so many fights this year? What are you missing?"

"Think about it thoroughly," Manav snaps. "Is today my fault? You are clearly confused here because you don't get that I am not responsible for what happened tonight."

Manav's mom intervenes before the shouting match escalates further. In a calm tone, she says, "I am happy you made it home safe, and I think your dad and I have many feelings built up inside from how your year has been." There is a short pause, then his mom adds, "You saw VJ with those officers this morning, and that may be your first time seeing that, but I have seen them get into trouble with the law several times. I'm not sure about the types of crimes he and his friends are committing, but we do not want you to end up down that path, so we are just worried about that."

"Exactly!" Manav's dad frowns, crossing his arms. "Pack up your videogames, too, because we should take that away for at least a month with everything happening."

Chapter Three

"Manav, I am glad you made it to my office for your appointment today," Maraino says as he meets him at the front entrance of his clinic.

Manav has officially returned to school since his altercation with Marcus, and he arrives at Maraino's office after his school day is over. Because of his incident with Noah, Manav primarily stayed home and did not attend any of his soccer or basketball practices.

"Come to my office to discuss the incident between you and Noah," Maraino says to Manav. "I received a report about it from Constable Rodney. To be truthful, I hope it did not create any trauma for you, and if it did, I want to inform you that I will support you as much as possible. How are you doing, though? And what did your parents say about it?"

"To be shockingly honest," Manav starts, following

Maraino, "I feel great after that situation, and it all turned out okay from start to finish. I was surprised that my dad was home that night, and he was initially angry about what had happened, but Constable Rodney clearly told him that I did not start the fight. But that only calmed my dad down just a bit, and he left town for work this morning."

"Your dad is a hardworking man," Maraino replies. "Is he able to get more time off work to support you during this difficult time?"

Manav and Maraino leave the front lobby to enter Maraino's room at the back of the office to discuss his incident with Noah. Before they do, Manav pauses to stare at the news network playing on the gray, staticky television in the corner of the office. He notices the news network that is playing is covering the housing crisis instead of the war, and the news anchor says, "The benchmark price for a detached four-bedroom home rises to one million four hundred thousand dollars. Also, inflation continues to rise as the cost of food, oil, and other resources increases."

Manav shifts his attention from the television to Maraino. "How can my dad take time away from work if everything continues to get expensive?"

Maraino hesitates, frowning, but eventually settles on an answer. "I understand it can be difficult to get by, but we will do our best to support you here. Let's continue to my room."

Manav takes his seat, and Maraino says, "As I mentioned, I received a lengthy report about Noah attempting to assault you."

"My heart was racing at the time of the incident, and I thought at one point that I would not make it out," Manav replies. "But out of curiosity, do you know what happened to Noah? I did not hear what happened to him after he left with the police."

"It says here that Noah did receive a charge for his actions from the police," Maraino tells Manav. "Did he really try to hurt you with the weapon he possessed that day?"

Manav nods and says, "Yeah, he did have a weapon. Luckily, I was able to maneuver around him and left without a scratch. I know nine times out of ten, things would've turned out differently."

"That is accurate, Manav," Maraino quickly replies. "A weapon always acts as a wildcard, and from my knowledge, him receiving an assault charge will create complications for him long-term."

Manav leans forward on the creaking metal chair. "What do you mean? What kind of challenges can it bring?"

"There are many challenges you could encounter with a criminal record, especially as an adult," Maraino shares. "Also, it can often lead one to commit other crimes, and you could spiral out of control before you know it."

They work through Manav's thoughts and feelings as the session progresses, and Manav gains some understanding from Maraino's comments about having a criminal record. But he quickly loses interest in the conversation and now looks forward to continuing with his day as his session with Maraino ends.

He leaves the office to go home, and after walking for a few minutes, he walks past his school and is surprised to see several groups of students spending time together on the school property after hours. He decides to walk across the street and enter a convenience store to buy a sandwich and water bottle, and once he walks out of the shop, he eats his meal and watches the students, surprised by their diversity.

He throws away the food packaging and empty water bottle

and walks home. After a few seconds, he hears, "Manav, make your way over here. Come here!"

Manav stops, turns around, and takes out his earphones to address the person calling him. He recognizes that the person attempting to connect with him is Nathan, a student at Manav's school. He is standing on the other side of the convenience store with a large group of people. Manav points at himself and shouts to him, "Are you talking to me?"

Nathan nods, waves him over with his hand, and yells, "Let's talk!"

Manav listens and decides to approach Nathan and his group of friends. Out of the multiple individuals that make up Nathan's social circle, Manav knows that he, Jairaj, and Kevin are the dominant players. Nathan shouts to one of his peers, "Move out of the way. Make some space so I can talk to him." His peer abides by his command.

Manav navigates through the enormous crowd and eventually stands next to Nathan. He pauses before interacting with Nathan first to make brief eye contact with the group, then Manav focuses his attention on him. "I don't think I have ever introduced myself. My name is Manav. What's up?"

Kevin intervenes before Nathan can reply. "What happened between you and Noah? And why did he get arrested and charged?"

Nathan places one hand on Kevin's left shoulder, looks at him with conviction and says, "I was going to get to that, so do not cut me off."

While Nathan expresses his frustration to Kevin, Manav wonders how they received information about this situation. "Noah and I were the only people in the alley that night, so how did you hear about that?"

"The word spreads quickly to many people," Nathan replies. "One person tells another, and next thing you know, it reaches multiple people that tell more people."

"That makes sense, but still confusing," Manav says to him. "There was a fight that happened between Noah and me. He had an issue with me fighting Marcus because I think they are related in a way, but I am unclear how. I think he was ready to get revenge that day."

Jairaj shows his interest in this matter by telling Manav, "That's good that you stood up for yourself. I heard he had a knife, too."

Manav continues to be shocked by the details Nathan and his group of friends are sharing with him. "How did you hear about the weapon? How much do you all know? But yeah, he did, and I'm just lucky to escape without an injury because the outcome could have been different."

Nathan, Kevin, and Jairaj continue with their questions and statements as they express their interest in Manav's altercation. Their comments include, "So you did not get hit with the knife? Because we heard he almost got you with it," "We also heard that you had a weapon," and "I heard from a few people that you are going to retaliate and plan to beat him up again."

Manav's confusion turns into a smile and laughter. "I guess information can spread fast, but so does misinformation."

"Are you calling us liars?" Jairaj accuses as he clenches his fist, his posture tensing.

Manav takes two steps away from the group to get some space and turns around to address them. "Somehow, someway, you know what happened that night. You have the main idea with some incorrect information in between, but we will leave it at that."

Manav gathers himself, puts his earphones on to listen to music, and leaves the large group to continue his typical path home. As he walks away, he immediately reflects on why Nathan is fascinated by his situation with Noah, and why his risk-taking behaviours resulted in him being appreciated by their group. However, as a person that generally flies under the radar, Manav did appreciate their praise as he had his feeling of being recognized somewhat fulfilled.

He reaches one of the intersections he usually crosses to get home. As he waits for the traffic light to indicate that it is safe to cross the street, Jairaj and Nathan power walk toward him as they leave their group back at the convenience store.

Manav removes his headphones and says to them, "Do you live this way? I have never seen you walk this way before."

"You take this path home from school?" Jairaj asks.

"Yeah, I am about twenty minutes away. I just like to head home and keep a low profile," Manav replies.

Nathan redirects the conversation and continues to bring up Manav's altercation. "That was brave, what you did to Noah."

Manav becomes fed up with them referring to this situation. "Yeah, I get that it all worked out, but I do not know why you are obsessed with it."

Jairaj gives his praise and justifies Manav's actions. "It's because you demonstrated strength by showing you are unfazed by anything that comes your way."

"Is that the true meaning of strength?" Manav says to him firmly.

"Of course it is!" Nathan shouts. "Manav, everyone around here is fake and weak, and, having said that, we could also use what you offer to help us handle some of the problems we are dealing with."

"I am not sure what I can offer you, but what issues are you coming across? Is it trouble with your homework or something? Are your problems related to sports?" Manav says to them.

"It's more important than that. It's something that needs to be addressed right away," Nathan replies. "There is this older kid, Vick, and I heard from several people that he is making false statements about us. There is a rumour that has been floating around that a few people have been stealing things from kids at our school, and he has been telling everyone that I am the one who is responsible for it."

"Dumb kid. I can't believe Vick would start talking like that," Jairaj chimes in as he raises his arms in frustration.

"Why does that bother you?" Manav replies. "Either ignore it or tell a teacher or the principal. They usually have my back, and I am sure they will have yours if you ask. Also, Vick seems pretty innocent. Doesn't he just play cards all day with his friends?"

Jairaj suddenly walks up to Manav and sizes him up, then grips him by his T-shirt. "You do not understand the problems he is creating by mentioning our names. We need to take care of it, and we need your help with it. We will have your back through it."

"Listen to Jairaj's words," Nathan says to Manav. "We will all be there, so you do not have to worry about the situation going sideways."

Manav becomes frustrated that Jairaj is speaking in a threatening tone while communicating his request to him. To calm himself down, he takes a couple of deep breaths, wraps his hand around Jairaj's wrists, and pushes it off his T-shirt. Manav tells Jairaj firmly, "Don't ever grab my T-shirt again," and slightly shoves him back.

Although frustrated, Manav sees an opportunity to earn acceptance from their group by helping them with this task. Therefore, to receive their respect, he decides to carry out this plan. He looks at both of them and says, "Alright, I can carry out just this one favour for you if you need it, and I will do it for the group. I will carry out a plan where I connect with Vick about these rumours. I will meet Vick by his locker when the bell rings for lunch and ask him about the rumours."

Jairaj, no longer frustrated with Manav, fills him with positive words by telling him in an energetic tone, "That's what I am talking about, Manav. I knew you would come through because you are one of a kind, the loyal type."

"Sounds good. It will all work out," Manav replies.

Nathan shakes his hand and tells him confidently, "You got this. There is nothing but loyalty in your blood."

Chapter Four

"I wonder how today will unfold. Hopefully, no one sees my fight with Vick, and if they do, then I hope I get away with only a little bit of trouble," Manav says to himself as he looks at his washroom mirror.

Manav does his routine before leaving for school, and as he brushes his teeth, he feels a sharp pain in his stomach and back due to the anxiety he feels about what will transpire at lunch with Vick. He heads downstairs to eat breakfast in the kitchen with his mom, and she agrees to drive him to school for his soccer practice early this morning.

In the car, he stares out the passenger window and reflects on the different scenarios that may play out when he carries out the plan Jairaj and Nathan have set out for him. He understands that carrying out their request will lead him into trouble at school, but if he fails to do it, he could lose the friendship he is attempting to establish with them. Because of the pros and cons of this situation, Manav turns to his mom and asks her for advice.

"Hey, Mom," he says to her. However, with hesitancy, Manav pauses and says, "Never mind, actually," because he knows she will have an unfavourable response about this matter.

He arrives at school after a short car ride and proceeds to the soccer field. As he takes a few steps out of the car, he sees Devin, but today, he is angry with his dad. With their car windows slightly open, he overhears Devin shouting, "Shut up!" to his father, then he steps out of his car, slams his door shut, and walks to the field. As a family that communicates well together, it's an unusual scene to witness.

Manav does not approach Devin immediately but instead gives him space. They are all on the field and get their soccer gear on, and Manav and his team begin their practice by running laps as their warm-up activity. He starts with a light jog and, eventually, sprints next to Devin, who is also participating in this exercise.

"I should mention, Devin, I have never seen you mad at your pops like that," Manav says to him.

"I would not look into it too much, man," Devin replies. "It is not always perfect between us. He puts a lot of pressure on me to stay focused on school and sports. You know, I did not do well in science and English last year, so he is on me constantly and checking in with my teachers to find out how I am doing with assignments and tests. It could be tough to deal with, and I have a busy schedule, but I take it day by day."

After a short pause, Devin adds, "Plus, handling the ups and downs of being a teenager has its own challenges. But like I said, you do not need to worry about it as we usually work it out together. What about yourself, though, Manav? There is a rumour going around that you want to fight Vick today."

Manav raises his eyebrows at him as they walk to the centre of the soccer field for their stretching activity. "How did you hear about that? I only talked about that with Jairaj and Nathan after school yesterday."

Devin has a short laugh and says, "It is hard to keep information like that a secret when you are our age. It generally spreads to many people."

"So I have heard," he replies.

Devin continues to question Manav about his actions. "Why are you planning to fight him? He seems innocent. He is just another kid that usually plays cards and board games at lunch, so I don't see how he could be a threat. I've also never seen you and Vick talk, so I don't understand why you would want to do that."

Manav takes a deep breath as Devin's brutally truthful remarks slightly impact him. "To be honest, I am not completely sure," Manav says. "Nathan, Jairaj, and Kevin praised me for what I did to Noah. They feel like I am capable of handling him, so I said I would do it today at lunch."

Devin is still puzzled by Manav's intentions of hurting Vick. With a confident, firm tone, he says to Manav, "That is still not a good answer and does not explain why you should fight him. Why would you try to hurt him, knowing it can impact yourself? If Nathan has an issue with Vick, don't you think he should take care of it? I just don't get why you are in this mix of this."

Devin's honest words continue to have an impact on Manav. He understands that he has already taken time away from school this year because of his fight with Marcus, and the next serious act he commits could have him no longer attending his school. Manav replies to Devin in a slow, hesitant tone, "They are embracing me, and I am doing it for them."

"That does not make any sense still," Devin says. "Nathan spends his time with thirty other people, so why can't he just get one of them to do it?"

Manav's worry because of Devin's remarks turns into anger. Therefore, he decides to take out his frustration on him. He stops participating in the stretching activity with his team and confronts Devin face-to-face. He grips both hands on Devin's shirt and shoves him to the ground with all his upper and lower body strength.

"You are a smart guy, Devin. How about you learn to shut your mouth?" Manav yells to him.

Devin lies on the field with pieces of grass across his face and dirt all over his clothing because of Manav's push. Devin slowly gathers himself and makes his way back to his feet. The entire soccer team stops participating in the stretching activity after they witness this situation transpiring. They rush in between Manav and Devin to ensure they do attack each other, but Manav and Devin do not show any signs of further escalation.

"You have completely lost your mind, Manav!" their coach yells. "Get your bags and equipment and leave the field now. You are not ready to be in practice today!"

Manav turns around and walks to his backpack, changes out of his soccer cleats and gear quickly, and is ready to walk off the field. Before he leaves, he looks back at Devin. "You have words that cut deep, right? Well, so do I. Look at you, Devin. Look at you. You are always spending time with your family or doing stuff that is not even relevant. Look at you, Devin. Who do you have with you asides from them? Exactly. Don't talk me out of what I'm doing." Manav then begins to walk off the field.

"Everyone, take a break!" their soccer coach shouts.

Although Manav leaves soccer practice in an angry, confident way, he immediately feels regret for fighting Devin. They have been friends since they were young, and Devin already came to practice after arguing with his dad, so this matter could make his day more challenging than it already has been.

Manav tries quickly to move on from this situation to focus on the task he must complete. He attends his first two classes, which are each almost two hours long. However, with many thoughts and emotions running through his mind, it passes by him in a blur, and the lunch bell rings. He puts away his belongings in his locker and goes to the cafeteria to meet Nathan. While walking there, he thinks about some of Devin's remarks earlier during soccer practice.

He enters the cafeteria, where he meets Kevin, Jairaj, and Nathan, and they begin to shower Manav with compliments.

"Looking big, Manav. You got this today," Nathan says.

"Looking tough," Jairaj adds. "I heard you got in a fight with Devin at soccer. We will have a talk with him for you."

Manav interrupts Jairaj before he can escalate the situation. "Everything we discussed yesterday about Vick will be done today, but don't you touch Devin. Have you seen him today? He usually grabs lunch in the cafeteria before he goes to tutoring."

"I won't touch him if you say so, and I have never talked to him, so I do not know where he is right now. I only heard you got into a fight with him this morning at soccer practice," Jairaj replies.

Manav raises an eyebrow at him. "Devin is one of the nicest guys around here. He is always helping around the school, so how do you not know about him?"

"I guess he just flies under the radar," Nathan interrupts. "Alright then, enough talking. We can figure this out later. Let's do what we need to do."

Manav, Jairaj, Nathan, and the rest of their group walk through the hallways to find Vick. With each step, the anxiety Manav feels in his chest grows sharper. Everything around him becomes quiet as he hears nothing but his short, pounding breaths and the sounds of his footsteps.

The echoes of Devin's truthful words from soccer practice this morning run through his mind. Although Manav does feel a connection to his new friends, he wonders why they are putting him in a complicated situation. He is eventually only a few feet away from making a final turn to the hallway where Vick's locker is located.

He notices when he is about to make his final turn that Jairaj, Kevin, and Nathan have slowed down, and he is now ahead of the group. This is surprising to Manav as he feels isolated in carrying out this act.

The group waits around the corner as Manav approaches Vick. They shout encouragements to Manav, such as "You got this!" and "You're the toughest kid around here!" One comment that stands out to Manav is when one of them says, "Your reputation is being built!" Making him feel like a soldier climbing the army ranks. However, in this case, he feels as if he has accelerated to the top of the pack of this group.

"Vick! I need to talk to you!" Manav shouts to him.

Vick gets up from where he is playing a card game with his friend. "Who are you?" are his first words to Manav.

"Does that really matter?" Masking his surprise at Vick's response, Manav raises his voice. "I heard you are spreading some rumours about Nathan and Jairaj, and I have a problem with that."

Vick looks back at his friend, who also gets up from the ground after playing cards, then looks back at Manav. "I have no idea what you are talking about. I don't talk to those kids. In fact, I don't remember ever saying a word to them. You didn't answer my question. Who are you?"

Manav is surprised that Vick is unaware of the rumours, and he becomes unsure how to respond. He decides to apply further pressure against Vick by continuing to speak in a more aggressive, escalated voice. "You know exactly what I am talking about, so you need to stop acting like you don't know what's happening!"

Vick then rolls his eyes at Manav and is speechless.

Manav looks over his shoulder at Nathan, who is peeking at the scene from around the corner. Nathan points his finger at Vick and says, "Get him now, Manav."

Manav nods and turns to look at Vick. He clenches his fist, stretches his right arm far back, and throws a vicious right hook that connects with Vick's cheekbone. Vick falls to the ground and lies prone, and most of the kids in the area yell and run away, while some run toward him to take photos.

Manav quickly turns around and leaves the scene by running towards the nearest emergency exit. He pushes the doors with full force and stops in his tracks as he sees his principal, Mr. Johnson, on the other side.

His principal looks over his shoulder and notices Vick on the floor, then he looks at Manav. "Walk with me, and let's talk about this."

He escorts Manav to his office to discuss his incident with Vick. When they enter the office, Manav sees a small, black television located at the back next to a printer. The television displays a news reporter interviewing an inmate serving several years in prison for an assault and theft charge.

The anchorwoman tells the prisoner, "It must be difficult being in seclusion for most of the day for all these years. What do you feel, and how can we influence others not to commit these same mistakes?"

The prisoner keeps his response short and direct by saying, "Being locked in a box all day has destroyed my well-being. This is my life now. My mom and dad visit me frequently, but many others have disappeared. It's important to be aware of what's happening in your environment. Your ego will pass."

Due to its poor connection, the television freezes, and Manav proceeds into the principal's office.

Chapter Five

"I made a crucial mistake today, and I don't know what came over me," Manav tells his principal.

Manav pleads with his principal about his incident with Vick as he hopes that he will forgive him. He tells him, "Nathan and his friends have been giving me praise for fighting Noah and wanted me to carry out the fight I did today, so I did that favour for them."

After a lengthy conversation, they agree that Manav taking some more time away from school would be reasonable because of his part in fighting Vick.

Manav walks to his locker and collects his things as he prepares to go home, and when he is a few feet away, he hears his phone vibrating against the metal frames of his locker. He opens it immediately, grabs his phone, and notices that the front screen of his phone shows that he is receiving notifications from a social media post that Nathan tagged him in.

"I wonder what he would post about me on his page," Manav says out loud.

He opens his social media app on his phone and discovers that Nathan uploaded a post that says:

@ManavJ You really gave it to Vick today. Well done.

Attached to this caption is an image of Vick lying on the floor after Manav's attack. After briefly looking at Nathan's post, he locks his phone, gathers his items, and walks out of the building to go home. He leaves through the front entrance, where he sees Jairaj, Nathan, and Kevin standing near the main road. They all turn around and approach Manav and show him appreciation by shaking his hand for what he did.

"You stood by your word," Nathan says confidently.

Manav nods, and before he can respond, his principal approaches all of them after overhearing their conversation. "You stood by your word? Is that what you are saying? All I know is that I have been informed of an unwarranted social media post. A classic case of cyberbullying." Mr. Johnson looks over to Nathan and tells him, "We should have a discussion in my office about that post."

Nathan walks inside the building with their principal while Manav shakes Kevin and Jairaj's hand. Before he leaves, Jairaj takes out a vape pen from his pocket and puts it in Manav's hand. He says in a low tone, "This will help the suspension go by quickly."

Manav looks closely at it in his palm, then places the vape

in his backpack. Instead of visiting Maraino, which he regularly does after his school day, he starts walking home and begins to self-reflect about today's event. Although he fulfilled his end of the deal in supporting Nathan and his peers, he has to suffer the consequences, and Devin's questioning of his group during soccer practice still replays in his mind.

He walks past an elementary school and pauses briefly to observe several children engaging in play on the playground. They all shout and scream as they pretend to be their favourite superheroes.

They all run around the playground chaotically. They fall and lift each other up, share their lunch snacks, and spend time together other as equals, demonstrating trust and unity.

"What am I even looking for?" he says quietly to himself. He turns around and continues his walk until he reaches his home. He opens his front door, walks in, and notices his mom watching television and drinking tea in the living space area.

"I have already been told about what happened today," she tells him while sitting on the sofa.

Manav places his belongings in his room and helps his mom with household tasks for the remainder of the day. In the evening, he sits on the window ledge in his bedroom and glances outside at the stars while Cooper lies on his bed. He decides to walk over to his backpack to take out the vape that Jairaj gave him, and then he returns to the ledge to experiment with the drug by inhaling and exhaling out of his open window.

He shifts his attention from looking at the stars and glances to his left where he sees two police officers approaching his neighbour VJ's home. They knock on his door loudly, and after several minutes, VJ finally answers. He looks around hesitantly with his hoodie on, appearing scared to step outside his home to address the officers.

"Curfew check. Just ensuring you are home. It's 9:00pm," one of the constables says. VJ nods just once at the officers, then he goes back inside his home and shuts the door.

Manav then leaps off his window ledge, lays on his bed, and scrolls through his phone. He opens his social media application to view Nathan's page and notices that his post about Vick has been removed. He closes the app and tries to call Nathan, but he does not answer his phone. He then tries to send him a text message, and although it shows he has read it, he does not get a response. This is a slight surprise to Manav as he thought Kevin, Nathan, or Jairaj would at least check in with him.

Manav locks his phone, puts it on his desk, and goes to bed. After roughly fifteen seconds, he reaches over to grab his phone again, unlocks it, and gives Devin a call. He is uncertain if he will answer his attempt to contact him, considering how soccer practice unfolded between them. On the fourth ring, just seconds before his call goes to his voicemail, Devin answers.

In a lighthearted tone, Manav tells him, "To be upfront and honest, I am sorry for what happened at soccer practice. I should have responded better in that situation, and I knew you were only trying to look out for me."

Devin laughs in response. "It's fine. You are just trying to figure it out with your own path. But, as you said, I was just trying to look out for you. I did not expect you to get mad like that."

Manav is relieved by Devin's light-hearted response when apologizing to him about their altercation.

"I have to get off the phone though to prepare for a few assignments and tests," Devin says, keeping his conversation short.

"How about we meet in the evening tomorrow at the Sunview Recreation Centre on the east end of Surrey for weight training?"

"I'm always ready for that," Manav confidently answers. "We will get a good workout in."

Manav follows through with Devin's invitation to lift weights at the Sunview Recreation Centre, and after spending some time at home, he returns to school the following week. He throws away the vape that Jairaj gave him, and unfortunately, he has yet to hear from that group. After reflecting deeply while away from school, he decides to prioritize bettering his performance with his academics and sports.

Manav walks to his locker on the second floor as he arrives back to school, where he sees Jairaj, Nathan, and Kevin standing. With a firm posture, Manav walks towards them and says, "Nathan, I messaged and called you a few times while I was away but didn't hear from you at all."

Nathan turns to him with a smirk. "You don't need to get angry without knowing the details. See, you are not the only one who got in trouble. My parents found out that I posted a photo of Vick on my page, and they weren't happy about that."

After hearing his response, Manav calms his tense voice and shoulders. "I didn't know that you got in trouble with your parents. Were they mad at you?"

"Well, I got some trouble for it," Nathan replies, smiling and laughing. "But I chose the right words, and eventually, I worked my way out of it with a small lecture."

Manav is surprised that Nathan did not receive much trouble for his part in the altercation with Vick, considering he played a crucial role in orchestrating that plan.

Nathan redirects the conversation by telling Manav, "That

issue is in the past though. Kevin is hosting a get-together this evening, and he's having us and some people from other schools coming, so you should join us. Are you in?"

Though he's surprised, Manav replies confidently, "I'll be there. Count me in."

Although he accepts their invitation to Jairaj's home, he is still confused about why they did not make an effort to contact him while he was away from school. He recognizes these acts are conflicting, but he ultimately decides to shake hands with everyone and keep his relationship with them on good terms.

Manav maintains a clean slate at school, and when the evening arrives, he looks forward to Jairaj's party. He shaves and wears his red and black Nike shirt along with jeans, white shoes, and of course, the chain given by his uncle as his only jewelry to go with his attire.

His mom gives him a ride to the party that evening and shows interest in Manav participating in an event with his new friends. "I am surprised you have plans today, Manav, but who are the people you will be spending time with?"

Manav keeps his answer short, hoping his mom does not ask further questions. "It is just a few people. That's it. Probably just video games or something."

"That really tells me a lot," Manav's mom says sarcastically. "Is Devin going to join you there? He would be a great person to spend time with."

"When does Devin have time for anything?" Manav replies, rolling his eyes at her. "But just don't worry about me. Everything will be fine tonight, and I will call you if I need anything."

Although Manav puts up a strong wall to prevent his mom from gathering more information, she continues to show her concerns. "I worry about those kids that got you in trouble. I barely know them as well. It would be nice if I could get their parents' phone numbers so I can get to know them."

Manav and his mom continue their back-and-forth conversation, and Manav ultimately does not provide her with further information about his peers.

He arrives at Jairaj's home after a short car ride. He steps out of his car and looks at Jairaj's large house, then he walks to the front door, grips the doorknob, twists until it opens, and enters his home.

Chapter Six

"A bigger crowd than I expected," Manav says quietly as he walks into Jairaj's house.

There are roughly ten to fifteen people moving from room to room after assuming there would only be about four or five individuals attending the event. He presses his palm behind the front door until it closes shut, and the slight noise from the door closing causes many people to turn their heads to look at Manav.

Manav pauses as he stares back, and he takes a few slow steps toward the living room to meet everyone. Suddenly, Nathan pops up beside him, puts one hand on Manav's shoulder, and shouts, "Manav! This is surprising. We did not actually think you would show up. Come meet everyone."

They move to the living room, where Manav sees several people lounging in different areas. Some people stand up from their seats and move to other parts of the room to make space for him.

"Big guy, I'm happy you made it!" Jairaj shouts when he notices Manav.

Kevin stands up from his chair to bring Manav a drink and food from the kitchen, and when he takes these things over to him, he tells him, "Relax tonight. If you need anything, then let me know."

Jairaj moves from his original spot to sit next to Manav. He reaches into his left pocket and takes out a vape and attempts to hand it to him. Manav shakes his head and puts his hand flat against Jairaj's right arm to reject the exchange. "I've got to cut the smokes out," Manav says to him. "I need to concentrate on basketball and soccer season, so I can't have that in my system."

Jairaj pressures Manav to accept the drug by saying to him, "It'll be kept a secret here. None of your coaches or teammates will find if you use it."

They go back and forth about him accepting the vape, but Manav ultimately decides to take it to not feel like an outcast. He inhales and exhales the drug, looks closer at everyone in the room, and says, "Is this what you guys do every week?"

Nathan laughs and says, "What else is there to do out there?" He then redirects the conversation. "Manav, what you did to Vick was impressive last week. You roughed him up, and he did not stand a chance against you. We need toughness like that to take care of other issues."

Manav continues using the vape and gives Nathan a firm look. "Yeah, I am strong enough to handle anything, but only if that involves taking care of myself. You, on the other hand, sound like you have your own issues with other people, so I wonder what you will do about it."

Nathan has a short chuckle and replies, "The real question is, what are you going to do to help us with it?"

After hearing this comment, Manav stands and stares Nathan dead in the eyes. "I am not fighting anybody else if that's what you are implying. I am not getting in trouble for anyone, and I am not doing any favours for you, so don't count on that." Manav then firmly grips Jairaj's vape and throws it across the room. He tells everyone at the party, "I don't need anything from you guys."

Nathan smirks, and Jairaj stands from where he is seated to grab his vape. He walks back to his spot, and as he begins to inhale and exhales the drug, he looks at Manav and says, "We respect your opinion, but you are acting like a loser."

Manav does not reply to his negative remarks. Instead, he walks away to the kitchen to grab more food and to meet other people as he feels unsettled by his conversation with Nathan and Jairaj. He maneuvers through the kitchen, moving side-to-side, as this area is full of other kids. He is able to grab a soda and a plate filled with snacks, and when he does a short turn to exit the kitchen, he bumps into someone, which causes him to fumble his drink. His pop can slips from his hand, and some of the dark drops from the soda spill on his T-shirt and floor. Many people in the area step away to avoid the mess, while Jairaj shouts from the corner of the room, "Better clean that up, loser!"

The last few minutes at the party have been frustrating for Manav, so he decides he will leave the event after he cleans his mess. He wipes down the floor with a wet and dry cloth, and he grabs a few napkins from the counter to clean his T-shirt. As Manav cleans his clothing, a random person holding a napkin in front of him places it on his chest to help him clear off the spills.

Manav looks up slowly to identify the person helping him, and he recognizes it's Anaya, a student that attends his school. Manav recognizes her reputation as a star athlete, excelling in both ice and field hockey, as well as being strong academically. She has a strong social circle and gets along with others. How does Manav know she is respectful, considering he has never spoken to her? He makes this judgement from his instinct, which he fully trusts in this scenario.

He straightens his posture to appear stronger and prideful. "You don't need help out with anything. I should be alright."

She refuses to listen and continues to help Manav. "Everyone needs a helping hand, so you can cut out the tough persona."

After cleaning him up, Manav extends his hand for a formal introduction. "My name is Manav. Nice to meet you, by the way."

She smiles at him and shakes his hand. "I already know who you are. We have had class every year together. You are not a stranger to me. I know that you play a lot of sports, too, and I admire how competitive you and Devin are when you are both competing against other teams."

"Much appreciated. Devin has upped his skills this year, and I'm just trying to keep up with him," Manav says to her. "You're an athlete yourself? I heard you are involved in ice and field hockey. I would have never guessed that."

"Never have guessed that? Do you think I am not strong enough to play such physical sports?" she says to Manav in a slightly irritated voice.

Manav is unsure of how to respond to her in fear of offending her further. Therefore, some awkward silence occurs between them.

"There is no need to worry, Manav," Anaya replies, bursting out laughing. "You are not the first one to tell me that. I get it all the time. Some say I should not play sports like that, but it's about having fun and breaking the norms, right?"

"That's a clever statement," Manav says, thinking about her comments.

"A very smart one, but now, let me ask you a question. You've been acting different this year with all of your situations at school, don't you think? Especially with your fight with Vick, I didn't expect you to be in something like that. Is there something going on in your life?"

Her questioning of Manav's behaviour reminds him of Devin's questioning during soccer practice. However, instead of feeling angry and upset as Manav did with Devin, he is moved by her approach.

"Sorry, that was too upfront," she backtracks before Manav can respond. "We can switch the subject. I'm not much of a fan of what happens here, and I know how these parties at Jairaj's house unfold as the night continues. You might be an incredible athlete on the soccer field and basketball court, but I'm sure I would be better on the ice rink. How about we do some skating at the arena at Sunview Rec?"

"That's my spot, and an invitation I gladly accept," Manav replies with a smile.

Anaya walks through the crowded kitchen to grab her bag from the table, and she and Manav make their way to the front to leave the house.

Jairaj gives him a smirk as he opens the door and is about to step out with Anaya. He shouts, "Not a loser after all!"

Manav and Anaya catch a cab to the local arena and arrive

there after a short car ride. They enter the facility and recognize it is a slow night as only a few people are at the venue. They gather their equipment from the front counter, strap on their skates, and take a few steps toward the rink.

As Manav plants his first step on the ice, he looks at Anaya and tells her, "Who would want to play a sport that is basically played in a freezer?" Manav slowly begins to shiver from the cold temperature, and Anaya replies, "You are overreacting. It will be ok. Let's do some laps around the rink to warm up."

They skate side by side periodically, and at times, they smile and make eye contact. Manav immediately recognizes that Anaya is a highly talented skater as the brightness of the lights glaring throughout the arena puts her skills on display.

They complete a few laps around the rink, then Manav turns to her with a confident look. "Alright, with the way you're gliding out here, I will admit that you have some skills. But right now, I feel comfortable after skating for a few minutes, and I feel confident that I am better than you at your own game."

Anaya raises an intrigued eyebrow and smiles. "Today, you can have an opportunity to prove that. Let's see who's a faster skater in a friendly race."

"I am up for it," Manav says to her. "How about this? We skate from one end of the rink to the other side and back. We'll do it twice, so do your best not to burn out after the first lap."

She agrees, and Manav and her line up along the goal line on one end of the ice. They stare at each other first, then shift their attention straight ahead as they are ready to compete. They press their skates into the ice with high energy and lean forward, then Manav suddenly shouts, "Go," and gets a head start as their race officially begins.

Manav completes the first lap smoothly and has a clear lead, and during the second lap, he looks straight ahead and feels confident he will win the competition. But for a split second, he looks over his shoulder and sees Anaya accelerating right past him. In an attempt to redeem himself, Manav presses his skate stronger into the ice in hopes of building more speed to catch up to her, but as Manav tries to gain momentum, his right leg that he attempts to push off loses balance, which causes him to slip and fall on the ice.

Anaya pauses as she sees Manav lying on the ice and shouts, "Give me one second!" then she turns around and skates to the goal line to finish their race. After, she skates to him and says, "I had to win the race first before I could come over here and help you." She puts her hand out and grips Manav's arm firmly to help him up from the ground.

Manav stands tall and brushes off the small pieces of ice on his clothes. He tries to hide his embarrassment from falling. "I was already sore today, but on a day when I am well-rested, you might not be as lucky."

After sharing a few laughs about their competition, Anaya and Manav agree to leave the arena. They change out of their equipment and wait outside the front entrance for their cab to arrive to take them home. The sky is dark, and the stars and the bright logo on the front of the arena shine over them.

"I have to admit, although I am competitive, you have skills on the ice," Manav tells her.

She shows appreciation for Manav's comments. "Thanks. My family really believes in me with anything I put my mind to. You were great, too, except for the part when you fell."

The minimal lights they are under shine on Manav's chain, which causes Anaya to comment. "I have never seen an engraving on a chain like that before, especially with the diamonds in the middle."

Manav unhooks it from around his neck and shows it to her, hanging from his hand. "My dad's brother passed this on to me. He supported many people on a farm he owned with the resources he has there. He always had this motivation to create something bigger than himself."

"That's meaningful," she replies. "But what I know is that diamonds on a chain like that are unique. Diamonds are rare. Diamonds are strong, like someone that's by your side through thick and thin."

Chapter Seven

"We will do cardio, then follow that up with weight training. Be prepared for a long day," Devin says to Manav.

Summer break has arrived, and Manav and Devin are spending time at the Sunview Rec exercising to better their skills for soccer and basketball season. Although Manav knows that Devin generally has a busy schedule, he and Devin are able to organize more time to spend together since they are on break from school. In addition to training together, Manav gets tutoring from Devin in English and math to help him prepare for his final year of high school.

Manav also spends significant time with Anaya during summer break as he makes her his official partner. They do many things together, such as visiting theme parks, restaurants, theatres, and more. Manav's connection with her continues to grow, and he goes as far as introducing her to his mom and dad, and his dad is incredibly proud of him for establishing a healthy relationship with her.

Manav did not have a positive experience at Jairaj's party, but he continued to associate with Nathan and his group of friends for the remainder of the school year as they still showed him respect. However, he keeps his contact with this peer group limited over the summer break as he dedicates much of his time to Devin and Anaya. Nathan has made an effort to contact Manav by calling and texting him on several instances during their break, but he is constantly ignored as he gets his voicemail or is left on read.

On his first day back to school, his dad drives him and tells him, "Manav, you did it. This is your final year of school, so please put your best foot forward to make it a good experience."

Manav nods at his dad and shakes his hand in agreement. He exits the vehicle, and as he starts walking towards the front entrance, he sees Nathan, Jairaj and Kevin standing nearby.

"Was your phone disconnected for the entire summer?" Nathan demands. "I kept getting your voicemail."

"Many things came up during the break. I was spending time with my family and trying to get ahead with math and English," Manav shares with the group.

Jairaj interrupts with a scoff. "Spending time with family? You mean hanging out with Devin and Anaya."

Instead of replying to Jairaj's remarks in what will likely be an unproductive back-and-forth conversation, Manav walks away from the group. He arrives at his locker to grab a few things, and Nathan approaches him alone.

"Something happened over the summer, and that's why some of us were upset outside just now," Nathan says to Manav.

Manav closes his locker and gives Nathan his attention. Nathan adds, "We were all together playing hockey at Central Park on the north side of Surrey. We were sitting on the side benches after we were done playing, just chatting and catching up. Out of nowhere, Vick's older brother came to the park. He has an intimidating look with his large build. He walked into the hockey cage and approached our bench, and he said to me that he wanted to talk. I agreed, so I walked and talked to him one-on-one. He took out his phone and showed me a screenshot of the post I had made about Vick, which of course, was already deleted at that time. He said he did not appreciate me hurting Vick and posting an image of him to my page to begin with. Then, he started to say something about payback being the ultimate satisfaction."

"Payback is the ultimate satisfaction?" Manav echoes curiously.

"Yeah!" Nathan replies. "I guess coming after me was his payback. He then grabbed me by my shirt and tossed me to the ground. While I was lying on the floor, he struck me a few times and made a video of it. The entire situation was embarrassing to go through."

Manav stands still as he is speechless after hearing about Nathan's incident. "It is sort of what I did to Vick," Nathan goes on, "but it's not ideal to have it come back to me. Anyways, that's why I called you during the summer. I wanted to see what we should do to get him back."

The first bell for school rings. "I'm sorry," Manav says. "I didn't know that happened to you. Hopefully, he will leave you alone from now on." He shakes Nathan's hand and continues with his day. While Manav attends his classes, he reflects on what occurred between Nathan and Vick's brother but wonders if he should feel guilt for not supporting him.

After the final bell rings, he meets with Nathan, Jairaj, and Kevin to walk home together. Before leaving as a large group, Nathan pulls Manav aside and whispers, "Before we go home, I want to let you know that Jairaj is still frustrated that you avoided our calls during the summer. He has some anger challenges. I think it's because he has trust issues."

"Should I address him about that?" Manav whispers.

"I would just leave it and avoid talking with him for now," Nathan replies.

They all leave the building together, but before walking home, Jairaj insists on first grabbing a meal from the convenience store across the street. They walk there together, and Manav spots Anaya as she enters her car to go home. He waves at her quickly and continues to march with his peers through the high-traffic streets.

Jairaj enters the shop and purchases his meal, and everyone waits for him to finish eating as they stand outside. Roughly fifteen minutes pass, and the traffic disappears as it becomes empty and quiet. When Jairaj finishes his meal, Manav asks everyone, "Should we all go home now?"

Jairaj throws away his food scraps, walks over to Manav, and tells him firmly, "We are not walking home just yet." Manav takes a few steps back as Jairaj enters his personal space, and he stares blankly at Kevin and Nathan.

Jairaj scowls at him. "You want to keep ignoring our calls?"

Instead of feeling uneasy, Manav does not back down from Jairaj's questioning and expresses his frustration. "First of all, I can barely understand what you're trying to say. If you feel that I ignored you during the summer, I already explained that I was busy during that time. But having said that, there seems to be a bigger issue to address here."

Manav turns his attention to Nathan. He points at him and yells, "If you were in an altercation with Vick's brother, and you were with several other people that day, why couldn't they support —"

Before Manav can finish his thought, Jairaj punches Manav in his temple, which causes him to instantly drop to the ground and become dizzy. He lays flat as he looks up to the sky with the shadow of Jairaj over him.

Jairaj shouts aggressive remarks to Manav, but he is unsure of what he is communicating. Jairaj then leans over and reaches for Manav's pocket to take out his phone and throws it twenty feet across the road so he cannot call anyone. The boys leave him there without a backward glance.

While lying on the ground, Manav feels the heat from the cement soaking into his back. After several moments, he scans his body, slowly regains consciousness, and stands to his feet. Although he took a strong punch, his ego taking a hit and his attachment to Nathan and his group of friends becoming broken hurts more than the physical injury. He looks at his fingers and toes and slowly starts moving them, and then he starts to move his larger limbs, like his legs and arms. Just as he thinks he is unscathed, he sees a bloodstain on the ground.

He slowly jogs across the street to grab his phone after it was thrown by Jairaj. He picks it up from the ground, unlocks it, and uses his camera to see his injury. He notices a cut and some swelling on the side of the head caused by the punch he sustained. He takes off his coat and presses it on the side of his head to prevent further bleeding.

Once Manav feels more stable, he gathers his belongings and begins to walk home. He reflects on his altercation with Jairaj and the mental effects he feels from this incident. More specifically, he begins to feel anger, resentment, and abandonment thought patterns, and he does not know what to do to help himself feel secure again.

His phone vibrates, and he sees Anaya's text: *Where are you? You usually call me right away when you get home.*

Manav does not reply and puts his phone back in his pocket. He makes his way through the alley where he and Noah fought last year, and he sees a 1990 Chevrolet Camaro parked at the end by the barriers.

Two people are standing by the driver's side smoking a cigarette, and they watch Manav as he walks by. Once Manav crosses paths with them, one of the individuals that has a scruffy beard and a scar running from the top left corner of his eyebrow to his cheek says, "Must have been a rough day today by the look of that injury on the side of your head."

Manav turns to him and shrugs his shoulders. "Definitely not one of the better days I've had."

"It is terrible dealing with people like that, to be honest," the stranger says to Manav. "Some people act like they're on your side but then turn on you the next. I know all about it. I went to school in the area and grew up here."

The stranger drops his cigarette to the ground and steps on it. "Take my number," he says. "If you want me to have a word with the people that did it, I will."

Manav is hesitant to take the stranger's number. However, after experiencing the incident he just endured with Jairaj, he decides to take his contact information. The random person gives his number to Manav, which he saves under a question mark in his phone log.

After a short conversation, they exchange their goodbyes, and Manav continues to walk until he reaches home. He enters his house, and his mother notices the red bruising and open cut on Manav's face. She transitions from shock to anger to calmness in seconds and takes him to the washroom to get cleaned up.

In the bathroom, Manav takes a seat on the toilet with the seat down as his mother goes through the cabinets to find anything that can assist him with his injury. She grabs polysporin, places the gel on a Q-tip, and applies it to his wound. "What in the world happened?" she says.

"Now is not the time to talk about it. I am not having it today," Manav replies. "They embarrassed me today, and I don't know what to trust anymore, so I must get them back. I am tired of this. I am tired of being picked on. I am done."

Manav's mom says in an empathic voice, "You have nothing to prove, so don't be so hard on yourself. Also, if you need help managing your feelings, meet with Maraino for counselling. You haven't visited him in a long time, and if you want to overcome this, you need to actively participate in those sessions."

Manav becomes fed up with his mom's comments, so he storms out of the washroom and locks himself in his bedroom. He lays in his bed for the evening. Anaya messages again and tells him that she heard about his fight with Jairaj, but Manav tells her that he is not in the right mental state to discuss it. Devin, on the other hand, pays a visit to check in with him. He enters his house and connects with Manav's mom in the kitchen, and then he walks upstairs to Manav's bedroom to meet with him. He knocks on his door and slowly enters his bedroom.

He shakes Manav's hand and sits on the chair beside his desk. "I see the injuries on the side of your head. This time will pass quickly, and this is all just temporary, so do not let this impact your well-being."

Manav, in frustration, tells Devin, "Thanks for coming over, but this is very complicated. I have to figure out a way to take care of it. Jairaj might get in trouble for his actions, but I know he is not the type to change. One way or another, I think he'll do it again."

"That's not the greatest way to look at it," Devin replies. "This time will pass. It may take days, months or maybe years, but if you focus on what is good for you, everything will be okay in the end. Also, if you want to join me in studying and weightlifting during lunch to avoid that group, you're always welcome."

"You don't understand anything right now," Manav snaps. "I was respected in that group, and now I'm embarrassed."

Devin stands from his chair, looks Manav dead in the eyes, and says, "You have some questionable connections, and you don't seem to be understanding that." He shakes Manav's hand to ensure that he knows they are on good terms, but he decides to leave as he is upset that Manav is not grasping his message.

Manav lays in bed while flicking his basketball in the air. He reaches over to his drawer to grab his phone, unlocks it and looks at the stranger's number saved in his phone log. He goes back and forth with the idea of calling this random person he came across after Jairaj attacked him. However, with the pain he feels to his ego, he decides to give him a call and sees what he has to offer.

After the third ring, Manav hears a deep, raspy voice that greets him on the other end of the phone.

"It's Manav," he says to the stranger. "I met you by your car earlier today."

"I remember you very clearly, Manav," the individual says. "My name is Arjin. How's the recovery coming along?"

"The physical pain is the least of my worries," Manav answers. "The war this situation has created in my head is what I need to take care of. Jairaj needs to learn his lesson."

"From the looks of it, they did get you bad. I can at least say I'd be pissed too if that happened to me," Arjin tells him.

Manav takes a deep breath. "That's exactly what I'm feeling. He needs to learn his lesson, but I don't know how to get him back."

Arjin, in a confident tone, says to Manav, "Just wait and see what I will do to help out, but the timing needs to be right. I'm familiar with the area as I am from the city. If you see them hanging out in the community, then let me know, and I will show up. I'll come by and have a word with Jairaj."

"What makes you believe that this will all work out?" Manav replies.

"When you have my word, you have my word. It will work out," Arjin tells Manav confidently. "But we need some favours in return. We have some issues we need to address with some people as well and things that need to be done. Just like I'll have your back, you'll have mine."

Without hesitation, Manav says, "Let's make it happen."

Chapter Eight

"Tutoring kids? This is how we're going to spend our lunch break together?" Manav asks Devin.

Manav gains the courage to attend school after his incident with Jairaj, and he mainly spends his breaks with Devin tutoring other students or weightlifting in the gym. He has crossed paths with Jairaj, Nathan, and Kevin on several instances in the hallways, but other than a few glares from them, they have left him alone.

"You spend your lunch breaks four times a week helping these kids, but they look like they're not making any progress," Manav admits, watching Devin tutor kids with their science homework in the library.

Devin has a short chuckle at Manav's comments. "To be honest, they are making some progress in understanding certain topics, but the improvement is definitely minimal."

Manav places one hand on Devin's shoulder. "Look, brother to brother, everything you organized here is great, but these kids are barely improving, even with the help you are giving them. Do you see the problem with this?"

Devin just laughs harder and tells Manav, "Some days can be more tougher than others when helping everyone here with their work, but it's about being consistent. It's similar to learning how to kick a soccer ball, hit a hockey puck, or shoot a basketball with perfect form. They all require practice and repetition."

Manav gives Devin a blank stare. Devin then adds, "I should also mention, although I am likely not the first person to tell you this, that you miss plenty of jump shots during basketball practice and games, and I wonder how you are often so far off target at times. But it doesn't stop you from practicing your skills to improve your craft. It's repetition and practice."

"I usually make about half of my shots, so it's not as bad as you say," Manav replies as his cheeks turn slightly red.

"I just hope you understand that point, Manav. If you don't, at least remember that if you're missing so many shots during our games, stop shooting the ball and pass it to me," Devin teases with a smile.

Manav finishes his time with Devin in the library and proceeds with his day. When his time at school ends, he stands outside watching Jairaj, Kevin, and Nathan walk home. "Today is the day," he says to himself.

He begins walking towards them and takes out his phone, sends Arjin a text and puts his phone back in his pocket. Manav follows the group as they cross the street, and they turn as they see that Manav is following them.

"Take a different route!" Jairaj shouts. "Walking this way is not for you."

"Nope, I feel like taking this path home right now," Manav says confidently.

"You're never the type to listen!" Jairaj scowls at him. "Use your big ears. I said turn around and figure out a different way home."

Manav does not listen to his threat as he glances at the group. Jairaj then slowly starts moving towards him, but surprisingly, Nathan quickly intervenes by stepping in front of Jairaj. He puts one hand on his chest and says, "Come on, man. Leave it alone today. You already got him."

This surprises Manav to see Nathan attempting to support him. "Why are you trying to have my back today?" Manav yells to him.

Nathan moves his hand from holding Jairaj back and turns to Manav and says, "He took it too far that day when he hit you. He was only supposed to talk to you about what was happening."

Jairaj gives Nathan an angry look. "I took it too far that day?" and shoves Nathan to his right side. Jairaj continues to move towards Manav. "The last punch I hit you with was just a warm-up, so watch what happens today."

Jairaj is chest-to-chest with Manav with his fists clenched. Nathan shouts to Jairaj from behind, "You are out of control," after being pushed by him.

Jairaj turns his head slightly back to Nathan and replies, "Keep it down. Better yet, shut your mouth completely."

Jairaj then looks back at Manav. He uses both of his hands to grip his T-shirt, lifts him roughly three inches in the air, and tosses him down to the concrete. While Manav lies on the ground,

Jairaj puts his foot flat on the side of Manav's cheek. "This impact will be more powerful than last time."

Jairaj lifts his foot, and Manav can only look from the corner of his eye and see the bottom of Jairaj's shoe with the sun in the background glaring over it.

Right before Jairaj strikes Manav, Arjin comes speeding in an Audi from the corner of the street. Jairaj moves his foot away slowly from Manav's face and watches the vehicle suddenly stop beside them. The car doors open, and Arjin emerges with two other tall men covered in tattoos.

Arjin lights a cigarette, and he and his two peers move toward Jairaj, Nathan, and Kevin. "Who's Jairaj out of you three?" he says in an angry tone.

Manav slowly gets up from the ground and stands next to Arjin. He points to Jairaj and says, "He is the one who attacked me. He was talking about doing it again today before you came."

Arjin and his peers walk next to Jairaj, and Arjin inhales his cigarette fumes and exhales it slowly, gently across Jairaj's face. He says calmly to him, "Not the tough guy now, are you?"

Jairaj does not reply, but his upper arms and shoulder areas begin to shake slowly because of the anxiety he feels from this situation. Also, he has tiny drops of sweat slowly rolling down from the side of his head.

"Staying quiet today, eh, Jairaj? This warning applies to all of you. Let's make this the last time I have to deal with all of you," Arjin threatens. He locks eyes with Jairaj and tells him, "Do not make me ever come back here again," then Arjin and his two peers walk back to their car and speed away from the scene.

Manav looks at Kevin, Nathan, and Jairaj, and he is surprised to see them in a fearful state. He strongly felt that they were a group that was fearless and unmoveable, but during that moment with Arjin, they appeared anxious and uncertain.

"Jairaj, you want to keep talking tough with me?" Manav yells to him.

Jairaj does not respond to Manav's remarks as he is still confused about the scene that just transpired. Jairaj then grabs his bag, gives Manav one last look, and walks home without saying goodbye to anyone. After he leaves, Nathan and Kevin approach Manav to clarify some of their issues. "Like I was saying, Manav, we just wanted to talk with you that day about what was happening," Nathan says to him.

"Jairaj took it too far that day," Kevin adds, "and it wasn't the plan for him to attack you like that."

"I understand what you're saying, but some things still do not add up here. If you both were worried about what happened, why didn't you intervene that day?" Manav asks.

Nathan empathizes with Manav's point-of-view. "It looks like we did not care about what happened to you from your side, but we didn't help during the fight and left with Jairaj because we didn't want to get in trouble for you getting beaten up."

After a lengthy back-and-forth conversation Manav has with Nathan and Kevin, the boys settle their disagreement with a handshake, and Manav resolves not to trust their excuses blindly.

Over the course of the next few weeks, Nathan and Kevin show more respect to Manav as they bring their friendship to reasonable terms, and they consciously distance themselves from Jairaj due to his negative attitude and actions towards Manav.

On a different note, Anaya and Manav's relationship continues to thrive. As a testament to their growing bond, Anaya takes the initiative to plan a special evening, inviting Manav to join her for a dinner where he will have the opportunity to meet her family. On the day of this scheduled event, Manav puts pressure on himself to make a good impression on her family. He wears the sharpest suit he has in his wardrobe and rehearses several discussion questions in the bathroom mirror to ensure a consistent conversation with her parents and younger brother.

After getting dressed, Manav's mom gives him a ride to Anaya's place, and when they arrive at her driveway, their eyes widen in astonishment at the sight of her luxurious home. Stepping out of the car, Manav adjusts his posture and proceeds to enter the front door of her house, which has been left unlocked, welcoming him to enter at his own leisure.

He takes his first few steps into her house and immediately notices the bright lights from the multitiered chandeliers that flash throughout the entrance, the pearl-white coloured walls and the polished, gray granite tiles. Anaya meets him at the front entrance where they greet each other, and she takes him to the dining area located on the other side of the main floor.

Manav enters this room with Anaya, where her brother, mom and dad greet him. He takes his seat at the large dinner table, and his evening with her family begins smoothly. Manav conversates with them about several topics, which include sports, movies, career plans, and deep conversations about their personal life experiences. When Manav shares that he is involved in basketball and soccer, Anaya's father shares his experience with sports and how it has impacted his life. He shifts his tone when he mentions that Anaya is contemplating quitting hockey, which is upsetting to him and surprises Manav.

Her father states, "She is embarrassed because she believes she's getting too muscular from playing hockey. She thinks if she stopped playing, then she would have a thinner frame like some of her favourite influencers. She has so many of them that she idolizes by trying to copy their physique and style."

Manav turns to Anaya as he becomes stunned by what he hears from her father. "I would have never guessed you've thought about quitting sports. You seem so fulfilled and confident with who you are." After a short pause, Manav adds, "Also, I wonder, if your influencers had more of a muscular build than you, then would you try to achieve that image instead? Or if they wore a brand that you didn't like, then would that even matter? Would you still wear it yourself?"

Anaya becomes slightly red as she is embarrassed. "Thanks. My Dad shouldn't have shared that, but I kind of get the gist."

With a short laugh, Manav expresses to her, "Whether you got the message or not, the main idea is that you should dictate what is valuable to you. Or at least make a logical judgment about what you are viewing online, first, and along the way, you might actually discover that you have the wrong influencers influencing you."

They change the direction of their conversation and enjoy the rest of their evening with the food prepared by Anaya. As Manav sits with them at the dinner table, his phone vibrates repeatedly. He takes it out from his right pocket just enough to see the caller ID on the front screen and notices it is Arjin trying to contact him. He calls multiple times, but Manav does not answer any of his attempts to reach him.

Roughly ten minutes go by, and Manav gets a text from Arjin: *Call me immediately.*

Manav does not want to ruin the flow of the evening, but he

also does not want to upset Arjin. He eventually decides to stand from his chair and tells everyone, "This is a lovely family and an outstanding dinner that has been put together, but I have to step out for a moment to use the washroom."

Manav walks to the restroom located on the other side of the main floor. Once he enters the bathroom, he places a large towel in the empty space between the floor and the bottom of the door frame to prevent Anaya and her family from overhearing his conversation with Arjin. He sits on the ledge of the bathtub and dials Arjin's number, and he answers on the first ring.

"What's up, brother? It has been a long time," he says to Manav.

"I'm just at dinner with my girlfriend and her family tonight. I saw your message about you wanting me to call you. Are you good?" Manav asks.

"Have a good time tonight, Manav," Arjin replies. "I wanted to check in with you to find out if those kids are still starting trouble with you."

"Yeah, it's a thing of the past," Manav answers. "But I don't know if they respect me as their friend or if they're just scared of me. It helped that you had my back in that situation, but what's up? What are you getting up to tonight?"

Arjin tells Manav, "Actually, I called because we need your help tonight just like we supported you, so you will have to leave your dinner shortly. One of my friends and I have these old prescription drugs that this old homeless person is willing to buy. He hangs out on Shackles Road on the west end of Surrey. Everyone in the area calls him Bones because he is skinny and looks malnourished. I've encountered him in the past. He can be unpredictable and uncontrollable as he loses self-control randomly, but he doesn't get physical, so he shouldn't hurt you."

There is a firm knock on the door. "Is everything ok?" Anaya asks softly, "You've been in there for over twenty minutes."

"Sorry, Anaya. The food was excellent tonight, but it is getting the best of me right now. Just another ten minutes," Manav replies. Once he hears her footsteps recede, he says to Arjin, "This task sounds simple. I just hand over the pills when I meet this person and receive the cash in return. This should be smooth, correct?"

"You have a full grasp of what you need to do. He will hand over about two thousand in cash, and you will receive some of the profits. We will give you the car when we pick you up," Arjin says confidently. "We will be there shortly, roughly fifteen minutes. You will be in and out of there quickly. Manav, we always got your back."

Chapter Nine

*"You were in the restroom for some time, Manav. I am
sorry if the food is making you feel sick," Anaya's mom says to
him as he arrives back at the dining space area.*

After a thirty-minute conversation with Arjin, Manav
returns to the dining room to rejoin Anaya and her family. Manav
smiles brightly at everyone. "No need to apologize. The food
was excellent. But I just got off the phone with my mom, and she
mentioned that Cooper, my dog, seems to be low in energy and
should see the veterinarian tonight. I have to get going now to help
with that situation."

"That sounds awful, Manav," Anaya's mom replies. "You
did not get an opportunity to finish your dinner. Before you leave,
I will pack some of tonight's meal in boxes for you and your
family."

"I will definitely take leftovers," Manav tells her. "I just booked an Uber to pick me up, so I should get going to meet them at the front of the house. It was an exceptional meal, and you're a gracious family."

Manav exchanges goodbyes with each of them, and he strolls to the front entrance with Anaya by his side. He gives her a hug by the door, takes a step out of the front entrance of her house, and says to her, "Thanks for organizing the dinner."

"Anytime," she replies. "We should do this again."

Manav nods as he agrees with Anaya's idea of scheduling another dinner event.

They stare blankly at each other, and Manav notices that she does not close the door to leave after giving her his farewell. She then shares with him that she will only go once the Uber driver picks him up, but this is problematic to Manav because he does not want her to notice him entering the car with Arjin. To persuade her to leave, he tells her, "You are polite for waiting, but it is getting cold, and you might get sick. You should close the door, and we will see each other tomorrow."

"I'm going to stay right here, Manav. Through thick and thin, remember?" she says to him.

"Yes, you said that when we went skating. I remember," Manav replies, giving her an awkward smile. "But right now, you do not need to be like that, and I will be fine."

"What is going on there?" Anaya's dad calls from inside.

"Manav has not left yet?" her mom yells in a curious tone.

Anaya is now joined by her mom and dad as they all stand at the front door waiting for Manav to get picked up. As Manav glances back at all of them, Arjin's vehicle, with its loud engine, comes speeding into the street.

"I am tired of these troublemakers causing so much noise in our area," Anaya's dad grumbles.

Arjin parks a few cars away, so he's not directly in front of Anaya's home. He has his arm hanging out the window with a cigarette in his hand and music playing loudly. Manav urgently wants Anaya's family to leave the front entrance so he can enter his vehicle without appearing suspicious.

Out of desperation, Manav turns away from Anaya's family, places his right hand on his left forearm and pinches with great force until a few tears come out of his eyes. He then turns to them with his head down to appear upset. He says to them, "Sorry, everyone. It is tough knowing that Cooper isn't feeling well. Do you mind heading inside to give me some space?"

Anaya angrily looks at her mom and dad and shouts, "Why are you all out here? Get back inside. You are all going to scare the only boy that has some interest in me away!" Bickering, the whole family shuts the door behind them.

"That was tougher than I expected," Manav mutters to himself. He quickly sprints to Arjin car and enters it.

"You came over dressed for tonight, but at least everything will be done in style," Arjin says as a way of greeting. "Bones wants the prescription pills in this brown paper bag. Again, he has an extremely thin frame. He is about six foot two, has thinning hair, and wears the same black jacket and green joggers all day long. Remember, he can get triggered quickly, so keep a safe distance. Do not ask him any questions and just grab the money."

Manav grips the brown paper bag and asks Arjin, "This won't go sideways, right?"

Arjin replies to Manav's question with one of his own. "You actually think I would get you hurt tonight?"

Manav does not respond to Arjin's question and agrees to complete this task for him. Arjin tells him they will drive to his apartment where he will be dropped off, then Manav will take his vehicle to meet Bones.

Arjin speeds through the streets as Manav looks outside the passenger window at the dark skies and the wind blowing heavily against the trees. He shifts his attention and observes Arjin driving and listening to his favourite tunes that primarily talk about expensive clothing and making money. He notices that Arjin sings along to the songs almost as if the messages in the music were his reality, instead of seeing that the words from the music are for entertainment purposes and are separate from real-world perspectives.

Once Arjin has been dropped off, Manav takes his car and speeds away to the west side of Surrey to meet Bones. As he nears Shackles Road, he dims his music and drives at a slow pace to avoid drawing attention to himself. He notices many homeless individuals on the streets that are either barely standing or walking, or lying in defeat on the concrete with the streetlights flickering over them.

Manav sees large garbage bags filling the sidewalks and grocery carts that contain random items being pushed by many of these poor people in this area. He reaches a red light where he stops and looks to his left at the front entrance of a pool hall. He sees an individual lying on the ground and slowly shaking from what appears to be an overdose, and no one is in sight to assist him.

Manav takes a deep breath and looks straight ahead. The red-light switches to green, and he continues to drive to complete his task. Manav takes a right on Shackles Road where he looks to his right and spots a person quickly pacing back and forth on the sidewalk while shouting out random remarks.

Manav stops his vehicle next to him and rolls his window down. "You must be Bones? Arjin must have told you already that I was coming to visit you."

This person glances at Manav, then suddenly sprints to the side of his vehicle. Manav is slightly frightened by his rapid movement, and as a result, he leans back in his driver's seat to keep a safe distance from him. He gives Manav a deathly stare with his rotten yellow teeth showing. "You got the correct person!" and walks away to the middle of the sidewalk and continues to pace along the street.

Manav opens his door slowly and steps out of his vehicle. "It's time for you to listen up. Like I said, Arjin mentioned you wanted some prescription pills, and I am here to give them to you. Let's make this quick."

Bones turns and stares at Manav and says in a chilling tone, "You are friends with Arjin, are you? You're a tall and handsome fellow, but to my eyes, which have never once lied to me, I see a rookie right through you. I see right through the poker face."

"Alright, now we're making progress with this conversation," Manav replies. "A rookie or not? How much does that matter? I just need the cash from you."

"Don't worry," Bones says. "There is no need to rush. This is how this this goes, and you're lucky because I love to deal with Arjin's friends rather than him. Where are the pills?"

"Let's get this done, and our paths will never cross again," Manav tells him. He walks to his vehicle, opens the passenger door, unlocks the glove compartment, and takes out the brown paper bag full of prescription pills Bones has requested.

"That's the package I asked for!" Bones cries as he stares at the bag like he's starving for it. "Stop wasting my time and give it here."

Frightened and uncertain about his unpredictable behaviour, Manav gives him the package of drugs. Bones opens the bag, takes a hard look at the items inside, then closes it. "Did I mention I love dealing with Arjin's friends? How did you not collect the money first before handing over this bag? I'm a bum! How can you trust a bum to give you money? Arjin has definitely sent the weakest friend he's ever had."

Manav becomes uncertain if he has made a crucial mistake by handing over the prescription pills before collecting Bones' money. To ensure that Bones does not avoid paying for the items, Manav says in a threatening tone, "Look, hand over the cash. Make this easy for me, and more importantly, don't make this situation turn out ugly for yourself."

"You're getting intense, Manav," Bones replies. "Relax. You'll get what you're owed. Plus, you will need that cash more than I do, and that means a lot since I'm homeless and have to sleep on cold concrete every night."

"What are you implying, Bones?" Manav challenges.

Bones takes a few steps closer to Manav until he is about half a meter away from him. He tells Manav in a deathly tone, "Listen, you want to make sure you collect your money." He takes out a half-smoked cigarette from his left pocket and lights it. He adds, "Do you think I was always homeless? I once had a good job. I was making good money daily and felt like a king in this world. My boss, however, talked a good game, but I was always suspicious of him. He would tell me he was proud of my work, but I knew he was jealous and wanted to get rid of me. Do you know what happens when the boss does not like you, Manav?"

"I don't want to listen to any stories," Manav tells him firmly.

Bones puts his hand in his coat pocket and presses outward an object that appears to be the shape of a firearm.

Manav quickly puts his hands in the air. "Look, if that's what I think it is in your pocket, just relax, and do not shoot!"

Bones chuckles and says confidently, "Do you know what happens when the boss is angered?"

Bones then slowly takes out his hand from his pocket, and Manav closes his eyes and turns his body as if he is about to get shot.

After several seconds pass, Manav opens his eyes and recognizes that he has not been hurt by Bones. He turns back around and stares at him, and recognizes that what he thought was a gun in Bones' pocket was only his hand coordinated in the shape of a firearm. Bones keeps his hand clenched in the same firearm position, with his fingers wrapped tightly in a fist and his index and middle finger sticking outwards at Manav. Bones tells him, "Just don't anger the one who trusts you, Manav. If you do, you will get fired." He then flicks his hand quickly, pretending to shoot a bullet.

Bones starts laughing loudly at Manav because of how frightened he became when sharing his story. Bones gives Manav the two thousand dollars that was promised in an envelope. Manav looks at the envelope for a moment, then looks at Bones and tells him, "I do not need to hear any of your stories. You're losing your mind."

Bones smiles at Manav after hearing his comments, then quickly vanishes into the night.

Manav walks to his car and drives back to Arjin's home.

During his car ride, he reflects on the comments Bones made to him. Although much of it sounds like nonsense, he feels he is able to piece some of his statements together and understand his message. Manav drives into the parking lot where Arjin's apartment is located, walks into his home, and sees him standing in the kitchen, waiting for him.

"Took you long enough to get here," Arjin says. "You were gone for just over two hours."

Manav puts the envelope on the kitchen table. Arjin walks over and opens it, takes out the cash and begins counting the money. "It took longer than expected, but you did what you needed to do." He then gives Manav a portion of the cash.

Manav takes it and holds it firmly. He then looks at Arjin and says, "Uncontrollable and unpredictable. You were not lying about Bones. He shouts and screams, then goes into random stories. He was saying a bunch of nonsense, like not to anger the one trusts you, and then he got into this story about a job he had once, too."

Arjin bursts into laughter after listening to Manav's experience with Bones. He replies, "That's why he lives on Shackles Road and will likely be there forever. Whatever that man says, just let it go in one ear and out the other."

Manav takes a deep breath and replies, "Yeah, yeah, you're right."

Chapter Ten

"You'll be going to the north end of Burnaby tonight where you will meet Manny. I've known him since high school, and he now owns a successful cannabis and vape shop with his Dad. But none of that matters because I never liked the guy, so we have to handle some business with him," Arjin tells Manav over the phone while he walks home from school.

For the past few weeks, Manav has had many nights where he is told by Arjin to settle disputes, sell different items, and commit thefts. To cover up his new lifestyle that involves many late nights out in the community, he tells his family he is spending time studying late at the library. When Anaya asks him about his constant exhaustion and the dark, shallow bags developing under his eyes, he tells her he has had trouble sleeping because of home and school pressures.

Arjin continues to provide more information to Manav about visiting Manny in the north end of Burnaby. "Their cannabis and vape shop is an established business, and we want some of that success," Arjin goes on. "At the end of each night, Manny takes home a lot of cash in a black backpack, and this is where we need your help. When he leaves his store and is carrying his bag to his car, we need you to blind him with pepper spray that we will provide for you. Then, you'll take his bag and quickly escape. If he tries to fight you back, you can hit him with some force, but don't hurt him more than necessary. He has family connections to people convicted of serious crimes that we do not want a problem with, so I do not want this situation continuing with him wanting any revenge."

Manav hears the details that Arjin has set out for him, but he does not reply. Arjin then calls on him for being silent. "You're worried about meeting Manny, aren't you? My friends and I always have your back, just like we helped you take care of Jairaj."

Manav calms himself. "I got it. It's for the crew."

"Of course you got this," Arjin replies. "I will meet you up the street from your school around nine in the alleyway tonight. It's a hidden location, so no one will see. I will give you my car then so you can meet Manny."

Manav fully understands the information about tonight's plan. Later that night, he lies to his mother by telling her that he will be participating in tonight's basketball game, which they do have scheduled for 8:30pm. However, he will be missing this event to meet with Manny in Burnaby.

He arrives at school late in the evening and enters the gym doors to watch the first quarter of the game before leaving to meet Arjin. His team and their opponent finish warming up, and they bring their starting five players on the floor for tip-off. Manav turns and sees Devin's dad sitting in the middle of the bleachers and decides to sit next to him to watch the game.

"Manav, you should be playing with your team tonight," Mr. Gill says to him.

"Mr. Gill, it's good to see you," Manav replies, shaking his hand. "I have to meet with a friend that needs some support tonight, so I'm just staying for the first quarter."

"Sounds fair but also not like you, Manav," Mr. Gill tells him. "I know sports are an important part of your life, and I know you would not miss the chance to play for anything. Also, you seem tense and exhausted. Have you been doing okay?"

Manav keeps his answers simple and direct. "Everything is working out this year. Everything is fine. I just have to support a friend tonight, and that's why I can't play and help my basketball team."

They continue to watch the game together, and the first quarter concludes. Devin has sixteen points and has completely taken control of the game effortlessly.

Manav looks over to Mr. Gill and says, "You raised a strong kid, Mr. Gill. He has a bright future ahead of him." He stands from his seat, shakes Mr. Gill's hand, and walks out of the gym.

He walks for a few minutes until he reaches the alley where he sees Arjin. He opens the passenger door and enters his car.

With an enthusiastic tone, Arjin's says to Manav, "Big guy, a lot of money to be made tonight from Manny. It's going to be good. This guy was super cocky when we were younger, so he deserves it."

"Ready to go," Manav replies in a calm tone.

Arjin gives him the pepper spray that he will use to blind

Manny when he confronts him tonight. He also provides more specific details about what he needs to do in order to complete his task. "Park at the gas station on Lamskon Way, which is roughly half a block away from his store. Once it reaches near 10:30pm, he begins dimming the lights in his shop, meaning he's closing. That is your opportunity to strike. You will leave the gas station and park on the side of the road next to his shop and wait for him to leave. When he takes his first few steps out the doors, ask Manny for the cash."

Manav agrees then drives Arjin to his home and takes his car to Burnaby, and as he reaches near Manny's shop, he reflects and realizes he feels more unsettled than usual.

However, he has little time to process his thoughts as he arrives at Lamskon Way. He parks his vehicle at the nearby gas station, steps out of his car, and has clear sight of Manny's cannabis and vape shop. As he has time to spare before Manny's shop closes, Manav walks inside the gas station to purchase a pack of cigarettes and a water bottle. He walks back to his vehicle, leans on the driver's side door, and begins chain-smoking in hopes of calming his nerves. He glances at Manny's shop located down the street and patiently waits until he sees any sign of him closing his store.

"That's a fine car you got there, son. What model is that?" a gray-haired man shouts to Manav as he stands by the gas pump.

"A 2015 Porsche Taycan," Manav replies.

The man smiles at Manav and nods at him.

Feeling good from this person's compliment, Manav decides to take his phone out of his pocket, opens his camera app, captures a photo of his car and posts it as a time-expiring picture to his social media page. Immediately, he gets many messages from his followers praising him for his nice vehicle, fulfilling his hunger for recognition. As he scrolls through his comments, he looks up and sees that the lights in Manny's cannabis and vape store are slowly dimming, meaning his store will close soon.

He drops his cigarette to the ground, gets into the car, and drives closer to the shop. He parks on the side of the road near his store, then steps out of his car and stands roughly twenty-five feet away from his target. He sees Manny walking out of his shop and locking the front door with his black bag in his right hand. Manny looks around to ensure everything is safe and begins walking in the opposite direction from where Manav is standing, and Manav immediately follows him.

Manav jogs until he is a few feet away from Manny and shouts, "Hand over the bag!" He reaches into his pocket, takes out the pepper spray, and presses the trigger in front of Manny.

Manny twists and screams in discomfort as he is blinded by the mist. Manav drops the can of pepper spray and attempts to grab the backpack. He gets a stronghold of his bag, but Manny does not let go and tries to fight off Manav to prevent him from escaping with his money.

As they both have a strong grip on the bag, Manny surprisingly draws a firearm from under his jeans and begins to shoot blindly all around the area. Manav immediately lets go of the bag, drops to the floor, and puts his hands on the back of his head to protect himself.

Once his cartridge empties, Manny tosses his firearm and runs away from the scene. Manav stands after lying on the ground and is undecided if he should chase after him. Then, he pauses and thinks about his connection to Arjin. He understands that if he fails to bring the money back requested by him, he and his friends could have altering views of him. Therefore, to avoid upsetting him, Manav begins to chase after Manny.

He sprints closer to Manny and has a clear sight of him. He watches him make a sudden sharp right turn into a closed grocery store. Manny breaks through the front glass door and runs inside to hide, and Manav slowly follows him. Manav walks straight along the front of the grocery shop with silent, slow steps peeking through each aisle in search of Manny. Manav pauses at the bakery aisle when he suddenly hears heavy breathing coming from the freezer section of the store. Manav then sprints to that section, where he sees Manny lying on the floor in exhaustion and excessively rubbing his eyes as he still feels the effects of the pepper spray.

Manav walks directly to him confidently and says, "This mess wouldn't have happened if you just cooperated. I didn't want to put you or myself in danger, but because of your actions, it led to this chaos."

Manav sees the black backpack lying next to Manny's hip, and he walks over to grab it. He opens it and sees many bundles of cash, then rezips the bag. He looks back at Manny and adds, "You should have just handed this over, Manny. You should have listened!"

Manav walks to the front of the grocery shop, and as he leaves, he steps across the shattered door. In his car, he takes in the sight of the destroyed storefront and says quietly to himself, "This is a mess."

Chapter Eleven

"You came through with what you needed to do," Arjin
says to Manav as he enters his home after his incident with
Manny.

Manav places the bag on Arjin's living room table, and he
and his friends that are with him begin to take out the money. They
give Manav praise for persevering through tonight's challenging
task. However, the positive reinforcement they give Manav
does not satisfy him today as he is still trying to comprehend
his incident with Manny. After spending an hour at his place,
they inform him that they will reconnect after his high school
graduation, which arrives quickly a few weeks later.

To celebrate his accomplishment of finishing high school,
he rents a suite in Vancouver at the Cavstros Hotel for himself
and Anaya, and Kevin and Nathan and their dates also join them.

Manav wears an expensive suit and organizes a limo for everyone. They meet at his home, but before going to their party, Manav first stops at Devin's house to deliver a few gifts. He reaches his home, walks to his front door, knocks it firmly, and is greeted by him.

"Devin, I'm hosting a party for some of us tonight to celebrate finishing school. You should quickly get ready and join us," Manav offers with a smile.

Devin looks over Manav's shoulder and sees Kevin and Nathan standing by the limo, then he looks back at Manav and replies, "I will pass tonight, but those are your group of friends that you should have a good time with."

Manav looks back at Nathan and Kevin briefly, then turns to Devin. "To be honest, you're not missing out on much by not joining us. I'm just having this party to celebrate our accomplishments, considering this may be the last time I see everyone. Before we move on to the next chapter of our lives. Anyways, before I head off here, I got a few gifts for you because who knows if we will be able to stay connected, too, especially since you will be busy studying while in university."

Manav gives a bag to Devin, and he takes out brand-new soccer cleats and basketball shoes.

"You're going to need it," Manav says to him. "Along with studying next year, I heard you made the university team for soccer and basketball, so these will come in handy."

Devin puts the shoes beside him and shakes Manav's hand. "Thanks for looking out, and I will put these to good use next year," Devin tells him. "Sports are temporary, though. It will eventually come to an end, and I will have to sort out my life after that. Right now, I'm still deciding whether to be a lawyer, a teacher, or something in the sports sciences."

Manav laughs and says to Devin, "If you're going to be a teacher, just make sure you don't annoy the next generation of kids like our teachers did to us. But giving these gifts is the least I could do. I can't thank you enough for always looking out for me, and it's always great to see how you're try to make a positive impact on others."

They share a brief conversation and exchange a hug goodbye. Manav gets back in his limo with Anaya and his friends, and they eventually arrive at the Cavstros Hotel. They enjoy an evening with drinks, food, and loud music in the luxurious two-bedroom suite that Manav rented.

They are all sitting around the living room table when Manav suddenly stands from his seat and walks to the balcony to stare out at the bright, flashy lights gleaming throughout the city.

Nathan joins him on the deck shortly after and says to him, "It's been up and down with us throughout high school, but despite our differences, I'm always with you, man."

Manav turns and shakes Nathan's hand. "Appreciate it, brother. It's good to know that you will be there."

Although Nathan went out of his way to give Manav some positive words, he wonders if what he stated was completely true. Also, he reflects on his desire for wanting a brotherhood and wonders if he found that in Arjin and his group of friends.

He walks back inside from the balcony into the living space area. Kevin looks at him and says, "Manav, we need more drinks and snacks. Can you run down to the hotel lobby and grab it from the vending machines for us?"

Manav nods and immediately leaves the suite and takes the elevator down to the main floor. He walks to one of the vending machines and purchases a few bottles of pop, then to another machine to get some chips and other snacks.

As he is about to leave the hotel lobby, his phone starts vibrating, so he takes it out of his pocket and notices Arjin attempting to reach him. After a few rings, he answers his call.

Arjin tells him, "Manav, we got to make time to celebrate you completing school, but I called because I heard you are staying at the Cavstros Hotel tonight. There's another party happening on the rooftop of that hotel with many other kids celebrating their graduation. Johnny, the one hosting the party, is wanting alcohol and drugs we have, and we need to give that to him."

"Look, Arjin, not tonight, man," Manav replies firmly. "I'm with some of my friends and girlfriend right now, so tonight won't be a good idea to do this."

"Manav, we've had your back through everything up until now, and you can rejoin your party after," Arjin tells Manav. "You will be in and out of there quick."

After some conversations Manav and Arjin have about tonight's plan of meeting with Johnny at the hotel's rooftop, Manav agrees to assist him with this request quickly, despite his lack of interest in this matter. Arjin drives to Manav's hotel and meets him just outside the lobby to give him a large blue duffle bag filled with illegal narcotics and alcohol.

Manav leans down to see his face through the passenger window. "Everything will work out with Johnny tonight, but after this, I have personal stuff that I need to sort out and will need space."

Arjin shakes Manav's hand as he understands his request, then Manav returns inside with the bag and enters the elevator to deliver it to Johnny.

"A very nice outfit for a special event," a short senior lady says to Manav, standing beside him in the elevator.

"Thanks," Manav replies. "Graduation from school. It only happens once, right? So I'm just making the most of it."

She smiles back at Manav, then gives him a look of curiosity. "You seem tied up with having drinks and snacks in your hands while carrying that large bag. Let me help you carry some things up to your floor."

Without permission, she attempts to grab hold of the strap of the duffle bag. Manav quickly drops the snacks and drinks and gently redirects her away from grabbing the bag.

"Very rude! I was just trying to help, young'un," she replies. "Your generation of kids have no manners."

The elevator doors open on the lady's floor. She stomps out with a huff, then she looks back at Manav and shouts, "Also, I was lying about your suit being nice!"

"That comment hurts, ma'am. I hope you have a nice day," Manav says as the elevator doors close.

Manav finally reaches the rooftop. The doors slide open, and once he takes his first few steps out, he is amazed at the massive gathering. The party has roughly fifty people, with music booming and colourful lights flashing brightly throughout the area. A tall man with medium-length hair sitting at a large table at the back of the venue makes eye contact with him and calls him over.

Manav walks over to him and has a seat, and he extends his hand. "My name is Manav, and you must be Johnny. Big party for you guys tonight," he tells him.

"You are correct," Johnny replies confidently as he shakes Manav's hand. "I'm surprised a guy like you knows Arjin. How long have you both been friends?"

Manav puts the blue duffle bag on the table next to Johnny,

and Johnny instantly begins to explore it. Manav tells him, "I met Arjin back in my city, and we have known each other for over a year."

"Arjin is a decent guy," Johnny casually replies.

Manav looks around and examines the people at the party while Johnny continues to look at the items in the bag. In a flash, Johnny grips the blue duffle bag and throws it with force at Manav. He is able to catch it before it drops to the floor, but he is unsure why Johnny is disappointed.

"I transferred the money to Arjin last week for this," Johnny vents his frustration to Manav. "But he fell short of what he was supposed to bring today. Honestly, it's not the first time he's done this, and I think it is time for him to learn his lesson. I think it's time for him to learn that he's messing with the wrong guy."

Johnny pulls out his phone from his pocket and initiates a video call with Arjin. He answers his attempt to reach him quickly, and he and Johnny begin conversating while Manav sits quietly and overhears their discussion.

"What's your problem?" Johnny shouts to Arjin to begin their conversation. "You pulled this stunt a few weeks ago and didn't pay me back for it, and now you're doing this again today?"

Arjin tries to explain that he made a mistake with what he needed to give, but Johnny berates him for his lack of honesty.

"Just give Manav the bag back, and he will bring it down to the lobby, and we will get it sorted out," Arjin tells Johnny.

Johnny draws a firearm from under his coat and points it at Manav. Nearby parties scream and disperse, and soon the whole room is in chaos.

"You will definitely get this correct right now," Johnny threatens, clicking off the safety on the firearm. "Because if you can't fix this or pay me back, then your friend is going to be missing a face in two seconds."

Manav's palms clam up as his mind races, trying to find a way out of this situations with as few bullets flying as possible. He eyes the heavy duffel bag and has an idea.

He looks at Johnny with a cool and unwavering gaze. "I have no idea what you're looking for, but this is an issue you can sort out with Arjin. I'm not going to be a part of this." Before Johnny can protest, Manav uses all his strength and throws the duffle bag at Johnny, which causes him to stagger and drop his weapon. Manav then dashes to the elevator and frantically pushes the call button to flee from this scene.

Glancing over his shoulder, Manav sees Johnny push aside the bag that he threw at him, grab his firearm from the ground, and fire one shot at Manav that grazes his shirt.

Manav then sprints for the emergency stairs, but as he shoves open the doors, he sees two men standing on the other side. Manav is surprised to see these people as he takes a few steps back. They flash their badges at Manav, and he recognizes that they are police officers.

"I am Constable Chester. My partner and I received a complaint regarding illegal activities happening here," this officer communicates to Manav.

Six other officers emerge from the emergency stairs, search the party, and arrest a few individuals. Manav looks at the sky as he hears a loud whirring noise. He sees it's coming from a police helicopter, its sirens flashing and an ample white light shining over the rooftop.

Constable Chester leans in so Manav can hear him over the helicopter blades. "What's your name? How old are you? And are you aware of any illegal activity at this party tonight?"

Manav gives him a blank stare. "My name is Manav. I...I just turned eighteen. I don't know what's happening right now."

"You're losing your memory about a party you just attended," Constable Chester replies. "Maybe your memory will come back when you meet Judge Chettinworth."

Chapter Twelve

"You need to cut him out of your life. Now that you're telling me about him, he sounds like nothing but trouble," Anaya says to Manav during dinner.

Manav was charged with drug possession during his incident with Johnny at Cavstros Hotel, and he set to meet with Judge Chettinworth the next day to find out if it would lead to him doing prison time. The night before he battles this case, he takes Anaya to dinner to be truthful with her about his friendship with Arjin.

"I saw Arjin as my brother. He has had my back through everything," Manav tells her.

"Yeah, he's your brother that puts you in a situation that will likely lead you to jail," she points out. "You told me at dinner at my house that I follow influencers who make me feel uncomfortable in being myself, but do you ever ask yourself the same question, Manav?"

He pauses for a moment before replying to process her comments deeply. He then says, "That's different. Arjin was still supporting me when other kids were picking on me. However, there's a bigger picture here that we can both agree on, which is that I need to make better choices. I want to go to university, just like you, and I want to get a job and live a fulfilled life. I don't need this young mindset anymore, but I need to make it through this case first."

"You're right. There is a bigger issue that needs to be addressed, Manav," Anaya replies. She puts down her fork and knife. "Looking ahead and understanding what you want to do with your life is smart, but the issue asides from this are your choices. Do any of these people like you for who you are, Manav? Nathan's come around to respect you, but you were only friends with him because you fought Vick for him. With Arjin, he seems to have your back as you say, but would he be your friend if you didn't do all this stuff for him? To be blunt, it seems like all your relationships are transactional. *I do something for you, and you do something for me type of thing.*"

Manav continues to think intensely about Anaya's remarks as they tumble through his mind. But instead of replying irritably, he attempts to shift her intense energy with sarcasm. "With that lecture you just gave me, you should reconsider that nursing program you are starting in the fall to be a life coach instead."

"We are not changing the direction of this conversation," she says firmly.

Manav takes a deep breath. "So, what if I keep hanging out with Arjin after this case is over and don't pursue my career plans?"

"If he is still in your life, then I would leave faster than a heartbeat," Anaya tells him. "That isn't something to joke about. We'll work together to get you out of this criminal charge, and then we'll see what we can do to help you after that."

"That's a smart plan," Manav says to her. "I actually have a career plan that I hope to work towards after dealing with Judge Chettinworth tomorrow. I am thinking of becoming a professional..."

"A professional what?" Anaya asks Manav as she leans toward him.

"A professional stay-at-home Dad," Manav confidently replies.

Anaya bursts into laughter after hearing Manav's answer.

"In all honesty," Manav adds, "staying at home for the rest of my life might be a good career for me. If I just want to watch basketball, soccer, and hockey all day while eating chips and drinking beer, would you be okay with that?"

"There might be some challenges with that, but we'll figure it out," she tells him as she chuckles.

Manav understands that this dinner could be his last with Anaya if he ends up doing prison time. Therefore, he continues to shift their serious conversation to a lighthearted talk for the remainder of the night to make this evening memorable.

Chapter Thirteen

The bailiff shouts, "All rise!" to everyone seated in the courtroom, and once they all comply, he asks those in attendance to take a seat so they can begin Manav's trial.

Manav arrives at the courthouse the following day to battle his drug possession charge, which could result in him doing either months or years of prison time, depending on how his trial unfolds. Of course, his desired outcome is to have his charges dropped altogether.

Judge Chettinworth takes a seat and begins to view the various documents detailing Manav's criminal offence. After scanning this information, he looks over to Manav, who is standing near the defendant's table. "May you please state your full name?"

"Manav... Manav Janjua," he says in a polite rasp.

Judge Chettinworth smiles, nods at Manav, and says, "It is

nice to meet you, Manav. According to these lengthy police reports I have in front of me today, you were spending a night out in Vancouver at the Cavtros Hotel with excessive amounts of illegal drugs. These documents mention that many officers arrived at the scene and were able to interview many people at the event. From the information they collected, most of the individuals indicated that the blue duffle bag filled with drugs belonged to you."

Judge Chettinworth continues to glance at the papers in front of him. He adds, "In addition to the police interviews, there are images here gathered from the security camera located in the main lobby of the hotel. These pictures show you walking in the hotel with that same blue duffle bag discovered at the event. With this information I have shared so far, do you have any questions?"

"No, I have nothing to add about the evidence you have presented," Manav answers firmly. "Honestly, it'll be difficult for me to refute your evidence. I was the one that brought the drugs to the party that evening."

Judge Chettinworth takes off his reading glasses, leans forward in his chair, and looks at Manav with curiosity. "Manav, I have to be upfront. There were many people with extensive criminal histories at that party that evening. Those people are in and out of the court system frequently. You, on the other hand, do not have a criminal record, and you appear remorseful for your actions by accepting guilt. You are only in your late teens and have your whole life ahead of you."

Manav sits quietly as he listens to Judge Chettinworth's lecture. Judge Chettinwoth clarifies his message by communicating to Manav, "What I'm trying to say is that, with the amount of drugs you possessed that night and from our discussion today, I'm wondering if there is more information to this story that you would like to share."

Manav slowly settles himself before responding to ensure he does not state anything that could be detrimental to this case. "As I already mentioned earlier, Your Honour, I take full responsibility for the drugs I brought to the hotel that night, and since I am admitting guilt quickly, I hope to avoid serving a prison sentence. But I will accept any punishment that you feel serves justice."

Judge Chettinworth gradually smiles and laughs. "You are really being discreet today." He shifts into a serious facial expression and says, "Manav, let me share a story with you. My youngest son, roughly the same age as you, had a hockey tournament in another nearby city many years ago. That night of his games, he had to take public transit as I had a great amount of paperwork to do. After his games were over, he was waiting to catch one of the two buses he needed to take home when four teenagers attacked him, and, unfortunately, they had a good crack at him. He was able to fend off two of the people as he attacked them with his hockey stick in self-defence. However, they were a large group and outnumbered him. He sustained permanent concussion symptoms that still affect him daily, and now has difficulty with self-regulation. The only good news is that it motivated him to volunteer in the community by helping others who have been victims of assault."

Manav is stunned by Judge Chettinworth's story. "I am sorry that your son had to experience that, Your Honour."

"There is more to explain, Manav," Judge Chettinworth states. "There were several witnesses at the scene when this happened, but many of them did not come forward with the crucial information they had. Because of this, we did not have enough evidence to prosecute the criminals responsible for this incident. And…"

"And…?" Manav asks, raising his eyebrows.

Judge Chettinworth adds, "And, Manav, when I view your case, I am wondering if there is any additional information you feel you need to share about the drugs you obtained that day."

Manav leans forward into his stand and locks eyes with Judge Chettinworth. "As I said, it was my decision that night at the Cavstros, and that's all you need to know."

Judge Chettinworth leans back in his chair. "If that's the final statement you want to give today, then I am willing to accept it. Considering the amount of illegal drugs you possessed at the Cavstros Hotel, I feel it is justifiable to sentence you to a six-month prison term. This is a significantly lighter sentence for what this charge carries, but I am considering that you don't have a prior criminal record and were honest for the most part today."

"A lighter sentence for what this situation carries is appreciated," Manav replies in a firm tone. "But as you said, I don't have a previous criminal record. I'm ready to move on from this and begin my life as an adult. What about doing community service instead of serving a prison sentence?"

Judge Chettinworth grabs his gavel and tells Manav, "I feel I am already being fair by giving you a short prison term for this offence, Manav, so I will stand by my decision. You will report to our local prison facility tomorrow morning." He slams the gavel down, stands from his chair, and slowly exits the courtroom.

Manav realizes his plea to Judge Chettinworth has failed, so he grabs his things and leaves. On his way out of the courtroom, his father, who watched his trial unfold, approaches him, places one hand on Manav's shoulder and empathizes with him. He tells

Manav, "You made a bad decision that night at the hotel, but your mom and I will be with you throughout this process."

Manav places his hand on top of his father's hand that is resting on his shoulder and nods at him in agreement.

On the day of his sentencing, Manav is expected to report to the local jail by eight o'clock. Two officers arrive at his home in a prisoner transport shuttle bus to take him to the nearby prison. They step out of this vehicle, stare at Manav's home, and wait patiently for him.

Manav bids one last farewell to his family and Anaya and meets the guards by the bus. They place handcuffs on him and seat him in the middle of the bus with other inmates who are set to serve sentences at the same jail. During the drive to the prison, Manav slowly dozes off while glancing outside his window.

The person sitting behind him leans into his side and whispers, "I hope I'm paired with you in a cell. I smell nothing but weakness coming from you."

Manav simply smirks in response and continues to look out his window.

The bus arrives at the jail located on the north end of Surrey. Manav steps out of this vehicle and takes a hard look at the enormous concrete building, and he, along with the other prisoners, are ordered by the officers to walk in a single file line as they enter the facility.

While walking in the hallways, many prisoners locked in their cells scream foul language at Manav and the new inmates.

"These metal bars won't stop me from getting a grip of you!"

"Prepare for a good beating, newbies!"

"I can't wait to turn you into my slave."

Manav remains calm despite the threatening choice of
words from the other prisoners. The jail guards briefly stop by the
cafeteria to show Manav and the new prisoners where they will eat
their meals. He sees that some prisoners have more food on their
plates than others, and he soon understands why as he sees some of
the more muscular, powerful prisoners steal food from those who
appear weaker.

After everyone receives a full tour, the prison officers
provide the new inmates with their mandatory orange jumpsuits.
Manav gets changed into this outfit, and then he is brought to the
two-bed cell that he will share with another prisoner. The guards
unlock and open the gates, and he immediately sees his cellmate
sitting upright on the edge of his bed with his head down. Manav
walks straight to the left and lies on the other available bed. He
decides not to address the other person until they address him first.
However, after an hour of pure silence, Manav clears his throat.

"What are you in for?" are Manav's first words to the other
prisoner. "This place probably ruins your life slowly."

The other inmate does not respond to Manav's comments
as he continues to sit quietly. Manav shifts his body position from
lying flat on his bed to sitting on the edge so he can look squarely
at the other person. He adds, "What do we do to pass the time
around here? Do we just play basketball and lift weights all day?"

Despite the other prisoner's unresponsiveness, Manav
notices a change in his demeanour. His breathing grows heavier,
seemingly triggered by Manav's words. "I guess I need to take

a step back on what I just said," Manav tells him. "You know, sometimes things can get real quiet and uncomfortable between people who don't know each other, so I get it."

This last remark causes this prisoner to escalate as he stands to his feet. He slowly walks over to Manav and sizes him up with his large stature.

"I wouldn't mess with me if I were you!" Manav warns. "I am well-connected in the community, and you don't know what I'm locked up for. I suggest you back up."

The man grabs him by the neck with his enormous hands and raises him from the bed. At six feet tall, he has Manav hanging in the air, then he pins him to the concrete wall, meeting him eye to eye. "I am not interested in any conversations while I'm locked in here, and I think you need a beating for all that talking," this prisoner says to Manav in a chilling, aggressive voice.

Manav cannot respond as the firm grip this prisoner has on his neck is obstructing his airway and, as a result, is preventing him from speaking. Manav then places both of his hands on this prisoner's arms and attempts to push them away from him. Unfortunately, this plan fails, then he scratches and claws at this prisoner to defend himself.

Manav gets a grip on his cellmate's sleeve while he tries to fight back and pulls down on it, creating a large tear. This prisoner looks at the rip in his uniform, then stares back at Manav. "I wouldn't have done that if I were you. You'll soon find out that I'm the most feared around here, and always expect me when you least expect it."

Manav realizes it is a losing battle as his arms fall to his sides, but this prisoner's words jostle a memory. He then looks closer at his cellmate and notices a blue, scribbled tattoo on his arm where his sleeve is torn.

With his last bit of breath, Manav shouts, "Noah, it's me! It's Manav!"

Chapter Fourteen

"Lunch time! Everyone stand next to your cell gate now!"
a guard shouts via the PA system.

Noah turns his head slightly when he hears this message,
then he stares back at Manav and releases his grip around his neck.
A guard stops at their cell, taps his baton on their bars to get their
attention, and says, "Leave the newbie alone, Noah. Both of you
get ready for lunch. You heard the message."

Noah and Manav stand at the front of their cell and watch
as their gates slowly unlock and open. Manav quickly glances at
Noah and sees him looking straight with his head high.

They get in a single-file line with the other inmates
and head down to the cafeteria where they fill their plates with
cold, hardly edible food like dry bread and stale, frozen cheese.
However, the last food item for the prisoners is a fresh, warm

baked potato that looks appealing enough to devour. Manav gathers his plate of food and sits in an empty seat next to Noah, but they do not converse as Noah focuses on his food and does not give Manav any attention.

They eat their meals when, suddenly, a muscular and heavily tattooed prisoner walks by Manav and his plate of food and steals his baked potato with his fork. He begins to chew on it in front of Manav and says confidently, "New man on the block. I'm Alphrez, and welcome to our party. We're always excited when we get new prisoners around here." Alphrez takes another bite of the potato and adds, "I will cut to the chase. You need to make sure you remember me because I run the show around here. I have to eat good first, and whenever you earn your stripes, you might be lucky enough to earn yourself a solid meal, too."

Alphrez reaches over and also takes Manav's cheese and bread.

Hunger gnawing at his stomach, Manav rises from his chair and grabs Alphrez by his shirt. He tells him, "New man on the block or not, I wouldn't try that around me. Not something I'll tolerate while I'm here."

While Manav confronts Alphrez, two of Alphrez's peers come behind him to support him, and Manav lets go of his shirt, recognizing he is outnumbered.

"Get out of here, Alphrez," Noah says calmly while eating his lunch.

Alphrez turns and looks at Noah. "Don't stand up for this guy, Noah. He's fresh meat, and you know what people like him deserve when they first get here."

"You heard what I said already," Noah replies. "Do you remember what happened to you the last time you didn't listen to me? Because I remember it didn't work out for you."

Alphrez is slightly frightened by Noah's threat, so he places Manav's half-bitten bread and cheese back on his plate. Alphrez then tells Noah, "You're always looking out for the new guys around here. You've got to quit that. You know, every rookie must face their bumps and bruises in here before they can start earning our respect."

"Why does it have to be like that?" Noah replies as he continues to chew his food.

Alphrez gives him a deathly stare but does not answer his question, and he and his peers slowly disperse from the scene. Several guards arrive at the cafeteria shortly after this situation to take the prisoners back to their cells. Once Manav is back in his confinement, he lays on his bed and stares blankly at the concrete ceiling, while Noah sits upright on the edge of his bed and stares at the bars in front of him.

Manav turns to him and says, "You had my back there. I don't know what these guys are capable of around here."

Noah, just as he has throughout the day, does not give Manav's comments much attention. Manav then sits upright on the edge of his bed. "I should address the tension in the room. I don't know if I should feel responsible for what happened during our fight in the alley when we were in school, but I will apologize for it. I'm sorry for what happened in that situation, but I was acting out of self-defense that day."

Noah stands and walks over to sit on the side of the bed that directly faces Manav. He tells him, "We were young kids back then, so none of that matters anymore. Unless you have any ideas that'll get me out of prison, then don't worry about it. You don't owe me an apology. You don't owe me anything." Noah takes a deep breath and adds, "This environment is tough. Everyone here lives with an attitude as if they have nothing to lose. They will punk you whenever they get the chance. You have to stand your ground because if they smell weakness, they will expose it right out of you."

"I'm starting to see that for what it is around here," Manav replies.

They lounge on their beds, hours slipping away as the jail settles and becomes quiet. Manav breaks silence and says, "To be honest, I remember seeing you hanging around in the community all the time, especially when it was late and dark. I don't think you came to school much, either. What was up with that?"

Noah gets out of his bed and walks towards the prison bars. He grips them with both of his hands and rests his forehead against them. From there, he peeks at a staticky, dark gray television mounted in the far corner of the hallway that is playing a documentary about an iconic life coach. It shows the coach walking through a large audience and empowering them with his words of wisdom. The famous life coach then chooses one of his audience members that is dealing with personal, traumatic challenges and asks her about her family dynamics and how it influenced her behaviour.

"They play this garbage on repeat all day," Noah shouts after viewing the video. "It's crap if you ask me, just like this entire prison."

Manav overhears the video playing, then looks at Noah and asks, "Do you have any siblings? Parents? How was your upbringing?"

Noah turns away from the television and looks directly at Manav. "My father took me under his wing after my mom left him.

However, it would've been better if he was not in my life, either. He was out of control and would drink a lot each night because he thought drinking would help him with his stress. But after taking down a few glasses, he would get angry, so I would try to stay quiet and nice all night to ensure I did not get on his bad side."

Manav gives Noah an intense stare while he explains his story about his family. "Damn. This entire time I thought you were just a big weirdo with a staring problem, but I didn't know you went through that. Do you keep in touch with your dad? And are you still affected by those situations you had with him?"

"He left when I was in the tenth grade, and I lived in different places after that to get by," Noah replies. "Am I still affected by that time, you ask? Not really. But he does show up in my dreams occasionally when I am sleeping in this dump."

"He shows up in your dreams? You mean nightmares?" Manav asks him.

Noah gives Manav a bright smile, then starts pacing back and forth. "He shows up in my dreams, but they aren't nightmares. When he shows up in my sleep, it's usually of him slowly creeping into my bedroom in our old house after he's finished drinking a bottle of rum. You better believe he is angry at this point after drinking that much alcohol, and to release his frustration, he would want to give me a whooping at the end of the night because he always believed that I was up to no good. So, as I hide under my blanket pretending to be asleep, he walks next to my bed, grips my blanket, and tosses it off of me so he can have a word with me."

Manav interrupts Noah from disclosing his story. "You said you don't really get nightmares of him, but this dream has the makings of one."

Noah grins at Manav and tells him, "Just wait. You see,

when he grabs my blanket and throws it off me, my little self is no longer there. Instead, he sees the twenty-year-old me. The six foot three and two hundred twenty-five-pound version of myself. He changes from a confident man to one that is terrified. I start to approach him with slow steps as he backpedals to the corner of the room. And let's just say we switch roles as he becomes the one who needs some discipline."

"Sheesh," Manav says with a shake of his head. "I thought you were a weirdo when we were in school together, and after hearing that story, it looks like I was right all along."

"Alright, Noah!" a guard shouts outside their cell. "Gym time in the courtyard. You know the routine around here. Just make sure you stay in your lane today."

Manav and Noah stick together for the remainder of the day as they exercise in the courtyard and sit beside each other in the cafeteria for dinner. They are placed back in their cells as their day concludes and lay in their beds.

"How much longer will you be serving time here?" Manav asks.

"Six more months of time left for a theft charge," Noah replies. "There's more to this than just surviving abuse from my father, which is shown by this blue ribbon tattooed across my arm. I also went from being a weird kid to being in crimes and wanting to fit in."

Manav gives a nod, and his eyes convey understanding. "I have six months in here, too, and this entire time I thought your tattoo was just a terrible scribble."

Noah gives Manav a sarcastic laugh as he is offended by Manav's comment. "You thought this tattoo was ugly? You do know you're as skinny as a toothpick, right?"

"You're correct," Manav says, smiling back at Noah. "The same skinny toothpick that took you out in the alley a few years ago."

"That was a few years ago. Do you need a reminder of what happened a few hours ago?" Noah challenges.

Manav and Noah get out of their beds and stand face-to-face with intense energy. Eventually, they smile at each other and shake hands to ease the tension.

"A few more months until we're out of here, brother," Manav tells him.

Chapter Fifteen

"You have ten minutes for your visit today. Do not go over the time limit," a guard warns as Manav is about to meet with his parents for the first time since being in prison.

Manav has served several months of his prison sentence and has not had any overly concerning challenges while in jail. Some of the other inmates, especially Alphrez, had intense, aggressive stares at him, but these situations have not led to any fights. He has not yet heard from Anaya and Arjin. However, he is excited about his first visit with his parents today.

He enters the meeting room after being escorted by a guard where he will get to connect with his parents in person. Once he sees them, he instantly shows that he has yearned for their connection by hugging them and telling them, "It's been tough without you two."

"This last little bit of your sentence will go by quickly," his mom assures.

They sit down and engage in a quick, casual conversation as Manav mainly asks them about their well-being and tells them about his experience in prison. He informs his parents that he shares a cell with Noah, and they are surprised to discover that an person he got in a fight with in high school would be partnered with him in jail. Their discussion is positive and smooth for the first few minutes but then shifts as Manav's dad shares that they have been victims of unusual crimes while Manav has been away. He elaborates by telling him that he has received threatening phone calls from unknown numbers, their vehicles have been broken into several times, and their home has been spray painted with cuss words and mysterious messages.

"You should have visited me in prison earlier and told me about this," Manav tells his dad in a firm voice.

A jail guard slightly opens the meeting room door and shouts, "Two minutes left!"

"Just keep it closed, and I'll be done on time," Manav tells him firmly. He turns back to his dad. "Were there any witnesses? Have you noticed anyone or anything suspicious around the neighbourhood?"

"I drove around the area and couldn't find anyone that could be responsible for it," Manav's dad replies. "I also spoke to many people in the neighbourhood, and they said they didn't see anything."

Manav leans forward in his chair. "To be honest, I was worried that this would happen. I did many things, even prior to what happened at the Cavstros Hotel, that led to me being here, and right now, it sounds like someone's seeking revenge. Some of the people I encountered are dangerous." He pauses to study the frown on his dad's face then adds, "For your safety, I think it's best you move somewhere else because they could be after either you or me. You can do this by asking Mr. Gill to sell our home, and once that's done, use the money you make from the sale and any savings you have to buy a new house in a different city. I also have the cash I made from this mess stored in a gym bag in the top left corner of my closet that you can use. Use the money however you need to, and we should act now."

The jail guard bangs on the meeting room door again and yells, "Wrap it up. One more minute!"

Manav acknowledges the prison officer's warning and rushes through the rest of what he has to say. "Look, you need to put this at the top of your priority list. I made this mess, and I am going to do everything I can to get you out of it. Again, this is your priority. Contact Mr. Gill to sell our house. Your safety matters."

Manav's parents inform him that they agree with his plan. He says farewell to them shortly after, and the prison guard enters the room to escort him back to his cell, where he sees Noah doing push-ups and sit-ups on the concrete floor. Manav walks to the left and takes a seat with his back leaning against the wall.

Noah stops his workout after noticing that Manav is upset. "You don't look too happy, dude. Did your family tell you you're dumb for being in prison?"

"That's exactly right, Noah," Manav sarcastically replies. He then stands from the ground and tells Noah, "I just need to make a phone call somehow, someway."

"Alright!" a jail guard shouts via the PA system. "It's that time of day. Gym time. Stand at the front of your cells, and we'll head down to the courtyard."

Manav and Noah stand at the front of their cells, ensuring they follow the directions of the jail guards, then, they, along with the other prisoners, are escorted to the courtyard for their daily exercise. As they walk through the prison halls to get to the courtyard, Manav glances inside the medical room and sees a black phone attached to the wall. He whispers into Noah's ear, and he looks back at him with a smirk and nods in response.

They are outside and ready to do some physical activity as several exercise machines are laid out for them to use. Manav and Noah decide to use the bench press to begin their workout. Manav uses it first as he lays flat and starts to unrack the bench bar with a wide grip. He holds it above him to start his reps when suddenly the grip slips out of his hand, causing the weight to plummet on his chest.

He shouts, "Help!" several times and many guards run to assist him. Noah intervenes by lifting the bench bar from Manav's chest and reracks it safely.

"What a softy Manav is, eh?" Alphrez shouts from a few feet away. "I hate this guy hanging around our prison."

Noah hears his remarks and turns around. "Stop acting like you're the toughest guy around here, Alphrez. Actually, now that I'm thinking about it, I should have taken care of you in the cafeteria when you were running your mouth. I think I will now."

The last thing Manav sees before he is carried inside by the guards is Noah swaggering up to Alphrez with his fists clenched.

Once Manav and the guards arrive at the first-aid room, he takes a quick look at the black phone attached to the wall. The guards lay Manav on the bed, then cut his shirt so they could examine his injury further. After looking intensely at his chest area, one of the prison guards says to Manav, "Where do you feel pain? I don't see any swelling or bruising anywhere."

"You guys are downplaying my injury, aren't you?" Manav demands.

"We're just having difficulty finding it," the guard tells him.

All the guards in the medical room with Manav receive a message on their two-way radios from the guards in the courtyard stating they need immediate support in de-escalating the fight between Alphrez and Noah. They tell Manav they will be back after they check on the altercation. As Manav watches them leave the medical room doors, he gets up from the bed and walks over to the black phone attached to the wall.

He lifts the phone, places it against his ear and says quietly to himself, "Usually have to dial nine first to get connected." He dials nine, then enters Anaya's number, and he recognizes that he is connected as the phone begins to ring.

"Hello?" Anaya says.

"Anaya, it's Manav. I'm calling you from the prison," Manav rushes out. "I want to talk and catch up, but I need to be direct with you right now. My parents have been victims of some crimes, and I have this gut feeling that someone could be after them. I need you to ensure they contact Devin and his dad so they can sell our house. There's a lot to the story, but I'll explain it to you later. Also, have you noticed anything out of the ordinary lately in your area?"

"Manav, it has been so long. I'll help your family out with that. Everything has been fine with me, but it has been different without you," she says to him.

Manav pauses as he hears the footsteps of the jail guards, signalling that they are returning to the medical room. "I'll talk to you once I'm out of here, but for now, just follow through with what I said by helping my family and stay safe."

The guards enter the room, and Manav stands from the bed. "You know what? I think you were right. After doing some stretching while you were gone, I realized I'll be okay." He then strolls out the door.

Their exercise time in the courtyard concludes, and Manav returns to his cell shortly after. Noah sees Manav and immediately asks him, "The prison guards that were helping you came outside. Did you make the call?"

"Everything worked out like a charm," Manav replies with a short laugh. "Anaya got the message. She said she's safe and that she would help my family with selling the house and moving. What happened in the courtyard? You stirred up a chaotic scene."

Noah smiles back at Manav and says to him, "Everyone here is weak. They actually believed you were injured. As long as I created havoc so you could have time to do what you had to do, then that's all that matters."

Chapter Sixteen

"You are out of here soon as well, so we will meet again, brother," Manav says to Noah as they shake hands and bid farewell.

Manav serves the remainder of his jail sentence, and he shares one last conversation with Noah as he is grateful for his support throughout his sentencing term. He then gathers his belongings from prison and goes to court to meet with Judge Chettinworth, as he will finalize his release.

Reading over his papers, Judge Chettinworth gives him a level gaze. "You were able to fulfill your conditions in prison while maintaining good behaviour. Your sentencing has been served. Any questions you have before you are set free, Manav?"

"No," Manav replies. "I am just ready to live out my life as an adult, and that can only be done by moving on from this situation."

He steps away from speaking to Judge Chettinworth and walks toward the exit doors of the courtroom. After taking a few steps, he sees his parents sitting on the benches, and they appear excited to see Manav free from prison. He stops walking, makes brief eye contact with his dad, then turns around and walks back to speak to Judge Chettinworth.

"I got lucky while I was in prison because I didn't face many challenges, but I know that's not the same for everyone," Manav says to the judge. "I came across someone I knew while serving time, and it made me realize that maybe not today, maybe not tomorrow, but maybe in the future, we can have more resources to teach coping and self-regulation skills to help those who deal with tough circumstances, and maybe it will prevent some of those people from engaging in a life of crime."

Judge Chettinworth takes off his glasses, stares directly at Manav and asks him, "That is a random thought, but do you want to elaborate on that idea?"

"I disagree. I believe you understood the message fully, Your Honour," Manav replies confidently. He then leaves the courtroom with his family.

He enters his car with his mom and dad, and during their car ride home, his dad tells him, "We were able to contact Mr. Gill, and he was able to sell our home. With the money we made from the sale and the funds you gave us, we were about to find a new place in a different city, and we managed not to have to downgrade in space. We must move all our stuff by the end of the month, so be excited for a new life in a new area, Manav."

He looks out his window as he has deep thoughts about his dad's comment. "Is it best for us if I move with you both?"

His mother, who is sitting in the passenger seat, turns her head back slightly toward him. "Of course, it's a good decision for you to live with your family. Considering you just got out of prison, how will you be able to live in this world without support?"

Manav takes a deep breath but does not respond to his mom. He and his family pull into their driveway shortly after, where he sees a large *For Sale* sign on their front lawn with a large *Sold* sticker across it. He steps out of their car, walks quickly to the front door of their home and opens it firmly. Although arriving home after a lengthy prison sentence and reuniting with family and his dog, Cooper, is rewarding, he immediately marches upstairs to his bedroom to contact Arjin.

He takes his phone from the top drawer of his desk and plugs it into his charger as it hasn't been active for several months. While it charges, he grabs his chain from the top shelf of his closet, cleans the dust off, and fastens it around his neck. He returns to his phone, which turns on as his home screen brightens. He sees all his missed notifications since the start of his prison term, but instead of addressing them, he dials Arjin's number.

"Welcome home, brother," are Arjin's first words to Manav.

Manav disregards his warm greeting. In an aggressive tone, Manav tells him, "You can cut the introduction. My family received many random calls, our cars were broken into, and our home was tagged with threatening messages while I was gone. I want to know why that happened, and I have a feeling you know something about it."

Arjin does not take kindly to Manav's choice of words and tone of voice. "I don't know what's made you mad since coming out of prison, but you should watch how you talk. I'm not responsible for what happened to your family, and why would I go out of my way to hurt them when I have shown you nothing but respect? You were the one who ruined the plan with Johnny at the Cavstros Hotel. Many people were arrested, and money was lost. All you needed to do was bring out the bag that night, and we would have sorted it out for him."

"He had a gun aimed at me and a clear line of sight, so how else was I supposed to react in that situation?" Manav snaps. "You have shown me respect for all the wrong reasons. And if you were always looking out for me, why not at least stop by the prison to check in? You had many months to do that."

"And if I came to visit you in prison, I would be surrounded by police officers, jail guards, lawyers, and others who are a part of the justice system, correct? Do you see how wrong it would be for someone like me to show up there?" Arjin emphasizes.

Manav is unsure how to reply, so he aims to end the conversation. "You know what? It doesn't matter if you didn't show up to the prison. You just go your own way, and I'll go my way. There will be no more nights out with you. No more fights. No more robberies. No more settling random disputes. No nothing. Don't even think about dialing this number, ever."

"That's a bad decision," Arjin says to him, laughing. "The people who threatened your family while you were in prison likely did it because of you. You need to understand that you made a lot of people angry, Manav, including myself, especially since you failed at the Cavstros Hotel. One day, someone out there will get payback, and don't be surprised if that someone is me."

Arjin ends the phone call. Manav scrolls through his phone and deletes his number.

He continues with his day and decides to put his last few years with Arjin in the past and make more positive choices that will help him through adulthood. He helps his family move to their new home, then spends his time applying to different universities and submits his resume to various companies in the hope of receiving employment. Fortunately, one well-established electronic store sends him an e-mail immediately after he applies requesting a job interview the next day, which he gladly accepts.

That evening, Manav contacts Anaya to inform her of his lifestyle change and sets a time to take her for dinner. They plan to go to the local mall first so Manav can purchase a new suit for his interview.

She picks him up from his house that night. "It's exciting to have you home, Manav. I'll do my best to help you get back on your feet and be there for you throughout this process."

Manav nods at her. "I just don't want to jeopardize my well-being anymore, and I'm ready to move on for the better."

They arrive at the mall and park their car. Manav reaches over from the passenger seat and gives her a hug to show her his appreciation for her help. They walk to the front entrance, and as they chat, another car strolling through the parking lot front tire pops, creating a loud, frightful noise.

Heavy sweating, breath coming in pants, Manav fights to suppress his instant fear and turns to Anaya to explain his reaction. "People need to learn how to drive and stop using these old broken cars on these roads."

They enter the mall and visit several stores as Manav searches for outfits for his job interview. He walks through many aisles filled with different styles of clothing but has difficulty concentrating on finding what he needs. Instead, he observes the people around him for any suspicious behaviour, such as those who are making intense eye contact with him, walking in his direction, or have intimidating physical appearances.

After Anaya finds an outfit for him to wear, he purchases it without trying it on as his anxiety heightens from being surrounded by many people. Exiting the shopping center, they make their way toward their vehicle, only to be met with an unexpected scene. A security guard stands by Anaya's car, diligently making notes on his pad. As they walk closer, their eyes widen as they see the driver's side window of Anaya's car smashed, and the trunk forcefully pried open.

"A lot of break-ins happen at this mall," the security guard tells them while causally writing his notes.

Anaya scans the car for further damages, and after doing a thorough search, she recognizes that the brand-name sunglasses she had in her glove department, and an expensive coat she had in her trunk have been stolen. She shares this information with the security guard, and she calls the police to file a report.

The security guard sheds more light on this situation. "We have information from a few witnesses that were in the area. According to their accounts, two men were seen around this car for a long time before they decided to break in and steal whatever was inside."

Manav's face contorts with frustration as he confronts the security guard. "Why would they choose this car, in broad daylight? Why not any of the other vehicles around here?"

The security guard sets his notepad aside, locking eyes with Manav. "Cause you had expensive valuables in your car that were easy for almost anyone to take, but unless you think it's from something else, then you can let us know." Pausing momentarily, the security guard scrutinizes Manav before his face lights up with recognition. "Wait a minute, I remember seeing you in the newspaper some years ago. Weren't you involved in the incident at the Cavstros Hotel?"

Manav avoids answering the security guard's question, then he spots two men about thirty-five feet away looking at him. He stares at them briefly, then turns and walks to the driver's side of Anaya's car and begins clearing the scattered shards of broken glass. After completing their cleanup efforts and sharing relevant information with the security guard, they leave the mall and cancel the dinner plans they had for the evening.

They arrive at Manav's house, parking in the driveway. "Hang tight," Manav tells her. "I just need a few minutes."

He hurries inside his home. After several minutes, he emerges with a suitcase filled with clothing and puts it in the trunk of her car. Returning to the passenger seat, he addresses Anaya with a sense of vulnerability. "Anaya, I've officially lost my mind, as you can tell from all of my reactions today. When that tire popped, I thought I was under attack. When we entered the mall to look for clothing at the different stores, I was looking at everyone instead of focusing on shopping as they all looked suspicious. And when we came across your vandalized car, it could be seen as just another case of theft to you, but I took it as someone that may be after me. Anaya, I'm telling you, I have officially lost my mind."

Anaya's initial reaction is a brief burst of laughter, but soon her demeanour softens as she empathizes with Manav. "I think you may be overthinking today," she tells him. "Not to disregard what you're saying, but I don't think anyone is after you."

Manav takes a deep breath, his words carrying a mix of vulnerability and determination. "I didn't tell you about this, but I spoke to Arjin when I got home from prison. I was mad about what happened to my family while serving my sentence, so I decided to address him about it. In that conversation, he threatened me because I failed to handle things with Johnny at the hotel. He also mentioned that I had made enemies before my time in prison and that someone might seek revenge against me. Those words have been echoing in my mind, and they might be contributing to how I've been feeling lately. I think from now on, I'll try to stay more reserved. To do this, I decided to pack my clothes and other belongings, and I will stay at a hotel on my own temporarily. I'll still go to my job interview, but this way, all of us are safe."

He pauses briefly, collecting his thoughts before continuing. "The good news is that you listening and supporting me has definitely made me feel at ease. You should still consider being a therapist."

"I will pass on that, but regardless of what you're feeling, you should definitely see a therapist," she replies. "Especially considering everything you've been through these past few years, they may help you cope with everything."

Chapter Seventeen

"Maraino, it's nice to meet you again. We haven't spoken since I was in high school," Manav says with a smile.

The hotel room is sparsely decorated, but the desk chair has proved comfortable enough for this video call. A glance at the clock tells him he has a few hours before his interview at noon.

Maraino smiles brightly on the laptop screen. "Manav! I haven't seen you in a few years, but I can see how much you've grown. How's everything been with you?"

"Maraino, I realized that I was not active in our sessions when I was in school, but I think I can use your support now," Manav says. "If I told you my life was great, that would be far from the truth. I have been bullied, hung out with the wrong crowd, and done time in prison. I, fortunately, have a supportive girlfriend now, but I don't know if we have a future together because of the trouble I've been in. I also want to move forward and embrace the next stage of my life, but my past choices continue to impact me. Right now, I constantly think I'm being targeted, and I worry for my family and what could happen to them. I also wonder why I made those choices in the first place."

"It sounds like you went through quite a few difficult events these last few years," Maraino says with a concerned expression. "When I hear about your bullying situation and that wrong crowd you spent time with, it reminds me of what you said to me when you were thirteen years old, Manav. It was the first time I met you, and what you said to me was –"

"I remember when I first met you and what I said to you," Manav says, interrupting him from finishing his thought. "I was young then, but I remember it clearly, and I wonder if that feeling has led me to where I am today. I said to you that I never felt good enough as a person, and it bugged me every day. I told you I didn't like who I was, and that I constantly tried to reshape myself to be more appreciated, but I was never able to figure it out."

"That's what you said to me when we met, Manav," Maraino replies emphatically. "I was surprised when you shared that. You were a star athlete, kind to others, and cared for your family, which you needed to give yourself credit for, but it seemed you wanted recognition and attachment in other areas of your life." Maraino takes off his glasses and adds, "But that was in the past, and we should figure out ways to support you now. To help you, it's important to understand how your thoughts, feelings, and reactions work together and how you can challenge them to change your perceptions. For instance, you mention you're upset with your past decisions. Instead of thinking of these experiences as negative times in your life, you can view them in a more positive light as they shaped who you are. I'm sure you have taken away valuable lessons from everything you have been through that will help you going forward."

Manav nods in agreement with Maraino's ideas. "I understand what you're saying when you mention my thoughts, feelings, and reactions work together. If I challenge my thoughts, then my feelings and reactions will change. That makes sense. I will take your advice more seriously now that I'm older. I'll apply the same effort I put into my physical health when I played sports to my mental health. I appreciate the help today, Maraino. We will see each other again."

Manav ends the video call and opens his internet browser to check his emails. He notices he has received a message from the manager that will be interviewing him today. This manager says they will no longer be proceeding with the interview after completing a preliminary background check of Manav.

"This is garbage! They couldn't even give me a decent explanation," Manav says out loud to himself as he reads the email several times. He steps away from his computer and begins to pace in his suite. "It's okay. Even though I didn't get this job, I can challenge this thought by understanding that there are more opportunities out there."

Manav then walks to the kitchen table to grab his phone and calls his dad to find out how they are doing with their move to their new home, and to ask him if he knows of any employment opportunities.

"Manav, my brother Robby in Toronto has several grocery shops that he owns. You could work for him," his dad tells him. "It will give you a chance to regroup with your health and get some experience. Since you have a criminal record, it could be tough getting a job out here, but I'm sure Robby will look past that and be accepting of you."

Contemplating his father's suggestion of relocating, Manav expresses his inner conflict. "I don't want to leave what I have here, but I also think this opportunity will help me get back on my feet."

After a lengthy discussion with his father, Manav decides to take this opportunity as it benefits him long-term and will only be temporary.

To break the news to Anaya, he brings her over to the hotel that evening for dinner. Shortly after she arrives, Devin, who just happens to be in the area, also visits him. They sit in the living room, but right before Manav breaks the news, there is a loud knock at the door.

Manav rises from his seat and says to everyone, "The final guest has arrived!"

He walks to the door, opens it, and says, "Welcome home, brother."

"It's good to be home," Noah replies. They shake hands, and Noah walks into the living room as he will be joining everyone for the evening. Noah takes a seat on the couch, reaches into his backpack, and randomly takes out a poker set.

"It's a great game that we can all join in on," Noah says to the group with enthusiasm. "Plus, if I'm being honest, I have a mountain of lawyer fees to settle, so I really need to start somewhere."

"You should consider better ways of making money," Manav says to him, laughing.

They sit around the table and play poker while Manav shares his news with everyone about moving to a different city.

"So, is moving out there your only option?" Devin asks. "Your parents are now in a different area. What makes you think Toronto will be better?"

"It could be better for me to move out there. It will allow me to work and develop some skills. Also, I think someone out here could be after me, especially considering what happened to my family while I was in prison and from speaking to Arjin." Manav pauses, then shifts into a firmer tone and adds, "Arjin said I've pissed off a lot of people, including himself, and they could possibly be seeking payback."

Noah extends his hand to collect everyone's poker chips. "Manav, no matter what decision you make, I've got your back. What I do know is that I'm already off to a great start after the first few hands we've played," Noah states with excitement in his voice.

"You're paying close attention to what I am saying," Manav teases. "Also, I didn't know you had lawyer fees to pay."

"Lawyer fees can be expensive, but so can tuition fees," Devin says as he intervenes. "Then, after getting that education, just hope that you can earn an hourly wage that'll buy you a home in this inflated housing market."

"The challenges of getting by," Manav murmurs. "On top of school and sports, you're also helping your dad with his real estate business and coaching at our old school? I could never get you, Devin. You have this drive in you that I never understood."

Devin looks at Manav with confidence. "You will get there too, brother. You will be better than ever once you make it through this situation."

Chapter Eighteen

"This won't be the last time we see each other, so I will say this farewell is only temporary," Manav says to Anaya in the lobby of his hotel.

After spending a long evening with Anaya and his peers, Manav walks Anaya down to the hotel lobby, where they exchange goodbyes as he leaves for Toronto shortly. He hugs her and watches her walk out of the building. Once she leaves, he rushes back to his suite to do one last inspection and gathers his belongings. He then returns to the main lobby with his luggage and takes a cab to the airport, and boards his plane to Toronto.

He stares out of the window and reflects on what his new life in a new city would be like, and how the unpredictability makes him feel confused. Manav's plane lands in Toronto after a three-hour flight, and he carries his luggage through several lengthy, narrow hallways in the airport and eventually arrives at the front of the terminal, where he sees Robby eagerly waiting for him.

Robby rushes toward Manav once he spots him and hugs him. "Welcome to our wonderful city, Manav!" They begin to walk to Robby's car, and Robby adds, "My son, we are unbelievably happy to have you stay with us. I think you will find this stay an incredible experience for you."

Manav smiles back at Robby. "This was a last-second plan, so I am glad to have the opportunity to be a part of your household and work at your stores. But how have you been? How's your family?"

They get into Robby's car and begin to drive to his home.

"Family is doing well," Robby begins. "Your cousin, Meera, has voiced many times how excited she is to meet you for the first time, and we will have a big birthday celebration for her tomorrow as she just turned four. We also have Shana, a relative from India. She has recently been living with us while she finishes her bachelor's degree here. Esha, my wife, has been busy as she recently opened her own clothing business. She also mentioned how excited she is to see you as she hasn't since you were only a few years old. I will introduce you to the stores where you will be working next week, so for now, just relax as you settle in."

When they reach Robby's house, Manav gapes at the size of it all. The home stands proud with its dark wood roof and stone accents. A tennis court dominates the space to the left of the main building.

"I didn't know owning grocery stores could buy a mansion like this," Manav says, marvelling in appreciation.

Robby walks beside him with his luggage in his hands. "There's a pool and basketball court in the backyard, too."

They walk into Robby's home, where Manav meets everyone at the front entrance waiting for him. Manav says hello to them individually and gives each person a warm hug. After, Robby gives Manav a tour of his home, which consists of several large bedrooms, washrooms, and kitchens. On the bottom floor, Robby shows Manav the suite he will be staying in.

Before he leaves the suite to give Manav time to settle in, he says, "I should be upfront with you, Manav. Your dad told me there was more to you moving in with us than wanting to work at my stores. He mentioned that you moved out here because you had trouble with the law and people back home. We understand that no one will ever make perfect decisions, and I will do my best to ensure you have a fresh start here."

Manav shakes Robby's hand to show his appreciation, then Robby leaves to join his family while Manav unpacks his belongings to get settled into his new space. He puts his things in the appropriate areas of his suite, then changes into his swimming trunks and spends time in Robby's pool in his backyard. He engages in swimming exercises for a few hours and sits on the edge of the pool to quietly watch the sunset.

"Manav! Manav! Can you push me on the swings?" Meera shouts as she and Shana are playing on the swing set.

Manav turns to her with a smile. "I can definitely help with that."

He walks over to the girls and spends time with them for several minutes. Suddenly, a loud slamming sound echoes from the other side of the yard, capturing his attention. He looks to his right as he is slightly elevated and recognizes that it's coming from Robby shutting the side fence.

Robby walks over to them with snacks and beverages. "We

have to use some force to close that fence as the alignment is off, so I hope that noise didn't worry you."

"It scared me a bit, but I don't feel as worried as I used to be back home," Manav replies as he takes a snack and drink from Robby. "I am working on challenging my views by understanding my reactions only occur because of my past, but I am feeling better now that I am here."

Following a meaningful conversation with Robby, Manav continues to spend time with his family and recognizes that this is the first time he has felt some tranquillity in a long time. As the evening arrives and the skies darken, everyone walks back inside, and Manav goes down to his suite to get ready for bed.

He showers and eats a late meal, then he lays in bed and watches Sports Centre on his TV to get caught up with football, basketball, and hockey news. As he is watching his show, he hears heavy rain filling the skies and sees flashes of lightning seeping throughout his room, so he walks over to his window and lifts the blinds to check the chaotic weather. He notices that the heavy wind is causing the swing set chains to rattle and the furniture to fly away from the patio.

Manav looks outside for several minutes when he unexpectedly sees three tall individuals wearing dark-coloured outfits standing on the other side of the fence. Considering it is pitch dark outside, he is unsure if they are looking at him as it is difficult to see. Therefore, he decides to run across his room to switch on the bedroom lights, then returns to his window and fully opens his blinds to let those strange people know he sees them.

However, when Manav peeks outside this time, no one is there.

He scans the area for any signs of suspicious behaviour,

and after finding none, he shuts the blinds, walks to his desk, and takes a seat. He brings out a few sheets of blank paper and a pencil from one of the drawers and begins outlining the names and physical characteristics of the people that could be after him and his family.

In the heading of the first sheet of paper, and for obvious reasons, he writes Arjin's name as one of the suspects. He outlines his physical characteristics below, which include being roughly six feet tall with a full beard, a medium build and a scar descending from his left eye.

In the heading of the second sheet of paper, Manav writes Manny's name. Considering that they got into a fight and Manav stole a large sum of money from him, he could be seeking revenge. Manny is roughly five foot nine, in his early twenties, with a few extra pounds, dark skin tone, and thinning hair.

On the third sheet of paper, Manav writes Johnny's name in the headline. After what transpired at the Cavstros Hotel, he could be coming after him as their feud led to them being criminally charged. He notes that Johnny has long hair, an athletic build, a light skin tone, and two full-sleeve tattoos that run from his upper arms down to his hands.

On the fourth and final piece of paper and for precautionary reasons, Manav writes Jairaj's name. Although his issues with him stem from secondary school, Manav believes Jairaj could be keeping a grudge against him. He is roughly six foot three with a buzzcut and thin beard, a slim build, and a slight hunch in his posture.

Manav puts the notes on his desk and examines them closely, ensuring he can recognize them in case he sees them.

Chapter Nineteen

"I saw some suspicious people peeking over your fence last night and looking at your home. What's going on with that?" Manav says to Robby while eating breakfast.

Robby puts his fork and knife down. "I've seen some people do that. They become amazed when they see our house because of how large it is, so they often stop as they walk by to get a glimpse of it."

"Sounds reasonable," Manav replies as he continues to eat. "But are you not worried about something happening to your home with many people continuing to eye it? You never know what their intentions are."

"You can take a deep breath and relax, Manav," Robby replies in a confident tone. "We have been living here for more than seven years, and we have never had any issues."

Manav simply nods as he feels any verbal response will lead to an unproductive back-and-forth. Once he finishes his breakfast, he rushes back to his room to get ready for the birthday celebration Robby has planned for his daughter. He does his hygiene routine and changes into a casual outfit, and, prior to rejoining everyone upstairs, he scans the notes he created the night before.

"I wasted an hour of my life writing this out. I'm overthinking this entire situation," Manav says quietly to himself. He piles the notes together, places them on the side of his desk, and runs upstairs to meet Robby and his family as they are ready to leave soon.

Manav reaches the main floor and sees his family standing at the front entrance. "What's with the all-blue outfits you're wearing?"

They turn around and stare at Manav, then he takes a closer look and notices the Blue Jays logo on the front of their shirts. With a smile, Robby says, "Get ready for a busy day today, Manav, because we're grabbing lunch downtown and watching the baseball game."

Manav is ecstatic. They leave the house shortly after to drive to downtown Toronto for Meera's birthday lunch. They arrive at a restaurant and enjoy their meals and drinks, and then they walk to the Rogers Centre where they are set to watch the game. The stadium is filled with a diverse, excited crowd, and they take their seats, which are only a few rows behind the field. The athletes participating in today's game take the field, and once they finish their warm-up activities, the game officially begins.

Manav is actively engaged in the match as several innings are played, even though he barely understands the basic rules of the game. At the bottom of the sixth inning, he video calls Anaya to share with her what he is experiencing, but she is happier to see him in a truly positive mental state for the first time since being released from prison. After a short conversation, he ends the call, looks over at his family, and notices their joyful energy. He notices Robby's heightened energy as he becomes louder and more uncontrollable from the alcohol he has consumed.

Manav taps Robby on the shoulder. "I will step out to grab everyone more drinks and snacks, and you can give me your keys. I will drive us home after the game."

"Good plan, Manav," Robby replies as he hands his keys to him.

After stepping away, Manav returns with food and drinks, and they continue to enjoy the rest of the game. Once the match ends, they and the other several thousand attendees leave the stadium. They reach their car and begin driving home but are stranded in traffic as many people leave the game simultaneously. As their car creeps down the road, Manav glances at Robby sitting in the passenger seat. He is fully asleep and appears exhausted. Manav shifts his attention to his rear-view mirror and sees Meera sleeping on Shana's shoulder and Shana resting her head on the window next to her. On the other end of the back seat, Esha rests her head on the other window.

While glancing at all of them, he notices from his rear-view mirror that the blue Civic behind him has its high beams flashing directly at their car. However, Manav gives little attention to this and focuses on his drive back to Robby's home. The traffic slowly eases, and Manav picks up speed and switches into the right lane to take the exit onto the highway. He notices the blue Civic with its high beams flashing follows him and maintains some distance to their car. To determine if their action is intentional, he swiftly switches lanes from right to left on the highway, and the car behind him does the exact turn and is only roughly ten feet away from their vehicle.

"I would not test me like that," Manav mutters as he eases down on the accelerator.

Robby blinks his eyes open and glances at the speedometer. "Moving fast there, Manav. Is everything all right?"

"You can go back to sleep. We're almost home, so don't worry," Manav replies.

The blue Civic following Manav suddenly speeds closer to him and begins to make light contact with his rear bumper. Manav tries to maneuver around this by driving his car side to side to avoid any further contact, but as he tries to dodge this car, they strike his car with intense force from behind, which causes it to first swerve uncontrollably between lanes, then spins hundred eighty degrees before coming to a stop.

Manav strikes his head on the window, and as a result, he becomes slightly dizzy and sustains a small cut on the side of his head. Robby and the rest of the family are awake with their eyes wide open and breathing heavily as they react to the event that is transpiring.

Manav and his family are now facing the front of the other car, and as Manav looks ahead through his windshield, he sees three tall men stepping out of the other vehicle wearing dark, baggy clothing. He squints his eyes to focus on their physical characteristics but cannot identify them as he still feels lightheaded from hitting his head.

One of the men standing by the front passenger side lights a cigarette and advances toward him while the two others wait by their car.

Manav continues to try to identify them as they appear familiar to him, and he suddenly hears one of the individuals standing by the driver's side shout, "That's him in the car."

After hearing this, Manav's anger and nerves give him the strength to unbuckle his seatbelt and step out of his car to address those people and prevent them from potentially causing harm to his family.

He takes his first few steps once he is out of his car but has trouble maintaining his balance because he is injured and fatigued from the car accident. He slowly stops walking and drops to one knee. While still glancing at the other person approaching him, he hears the sounds of sirens and recognizes that several police cars and ambulances are speeding to the scene. Manav turns around and stares at the emergency cars, then he turns back and sees the three men sprint diagonally across the street into a dark forestry trail to escape this situation.

The responders swiftly arrive, offering their assistance and support to Manav and his family. After being thoroughly examined by the medical team for any injuries and providing their statement to the police regarding the incident, they drive back home in their partially damaged car.

They return to Robby's home and sit in his living space area to debrief this incident. As Robby pours himself a glass of rum, he reassures everyone, "I understand that everyone is scared, but it was just a car accident, and I believe everything will be alright."

"It was more than an accident," Manav says in an angry, firm tone. "I was lightheaded after the collision, but when I got out of the car and approached those people, I thought I recognized one of them standing by the driver's side. But it was still difficult to tell."

"That could be a reasonable explanation for this, but it seems more likely that it was just a car accident," Robby says as he casually sips his beverage. "And maybe they took off from the scene because they were just scared of speaking to the police."

Manav silently nods in acknowledgment of Robby's words, but he internally disagrees with his perspective on the situation. As he continues to think about the car collision, he glances at Robby and says, "By the way, you've been drinking since lunch, maybe it's time to set the glass aside?"

Before Robby can answer, Esha interrupts, "Do not mind him, Manav. He generally drinks more when he is in stressful situations. He was getting better with controlling this, but ever since Robby and your dad's older brother passed away, it has made his battle with alcohol more difficult to overcome."

Manav turns to her. "I understand his passing was tough for us, but challenges like this happen to everyone. You guys have a great family and gorgeous home, and Dad tells me you make north of half a million dollars each year." Manav pauses, reconsidering his words. "But I guess money doesn't take away the stress, though, but I'm sure drinking doesn't either."

Robby slowly puts his glass on the table. Manav tells everyone, "I'm going to call my Dad tomorrow to check in on them and figure out another place to stay. I don't know if I'm overthinking this, but there is a lot of uncertainty if I stay here, especially considering what happened today."

"I hate living out here, too!" Shana chimes in from the corner of the room, her voice filled with conviction. "I either want to move back to India or go back to my uncle's farm and help everyone there."

"I've heard about Uncle Arvin's farm," Manav tells her. "It's in a small town called the Reveria Valley?"

"Yes. Just an eight-hour drive away from here," Shana replies. "He supports many newcomers that need work and a place to stay as it's tough to adjust here."

Manav holds the necklace around his neck with a tight grip, then smiles. "I think I have an idea."

Chapter Twenty

"The police are working hard to identify the people that hit our car on Meera's birthday," Robby says to Manav as he stands in front of his home. *"They said that the car those strangers drove was stolen and will do what they can to make sure we are safe, so I still think you should stay with us."*

Manav packs the items he has in Robby's home and decides he will live on Arvin's farm because it is in a discreet location where he will be safe. Before he takes his eight-hour cab ride to the Reveria Valley, Robby tries to convince him to stay in his home.

"Are you sure this is what you want to do?" Robby asks him.

"This is what needs to happen and it will all work out," Manav explains, remaining firm with his decision. After their lengthy conversation, they exchange their final goodbyes. Manav takes his belongings, and before he enters his cab, he quickly scans the front street of Robby's home to ensure no one will follow him. Once he sees no one suspicious in the area, he enters the car and is set for his trip.

"You are going to Reveria Valley? One of the most beautiful places in the world," the taxi driver says to Manav.

As the hours pass by, Manav engages in conversation with the cab driver and dozes off for several short naps during the trip. After a long drive, they approach the town of Reveria Valley, and Manav glances at the giant trees, various outdoor markets, and heavy traffic in this small town. "This is a really different setting than what I experience at home," Manav tells the driver.

"It's a lot to take in, but just accept it for what it is, Manav. There is such a large community for you to get to know," the driver replies.

The cab driver speeds and swerves through many streets to get to Arvin's farm, then they take a sharp right turn into a bumpy, gravel road. "Hold on tight, Manav, just a few more minutes until we're there!" the cab driver yells to him.

Manav glances out the window and sees cattle, chickens, pigs, and goats, moving gracefully across the agricultural land. Manav turns his head and looks outside the other window and sees various crops being grown and harvested by farmers, such as wheat, rice, and all kinds of vegetables and fruits.

Suddenly, the taxi driver presses the brakes and stops in front of a large farmhouse.

"I remember seeing this place when I was young," the taxi driver says to Manav. "I am still amazed by this area as I have never seen such a large farm in my life. I remember hearing stories about your uncle working tirelessly to help everyone here."

Manav does not reply as he is still mesmerized by the land. He opens the door, steps out of the car, and stares at the large house with people standing at the front. He reaches into his pocket to take out his wallet and gives the cab driver a few hundred-dollar bills for his service. The cab driver accepts the cash and leaves the scene.

A man standing at the front of the house walks towards Manav and sticks his hand out to give him a handshake. "My name is Neel," he says to Manav. "I help manage the farm all year around, and we are happy to finally meet you. Arvin created something special here. Let's get your luggage inside, and I will give you a tour of the area."

Manav shakes Neel's hand. "A tour would help me understand what this place is all about."

The other people standing by the house take his luggage into their home while Manav and Neel get into a large gray van to tour the farm. Neel drives him to several different locations on the farm to introduce Manav to farm workers and show him how they manage their crops and animals. Many of the workers are surprised to meet Manav as they know he is related to Arvin and understand his role in establishing this agricultural land.

Manav and Neel commute to different parts of the farm for a few hours, checking on crops and livestock and ensuring everything is running smoothly. As they drive along the bumpy dirt roads, Manav turns to Neel and tells him, "This place is incredible. It's large, and many of the workers seem motivated, but some of the buildings and equipment are outdated and broken."

Neel firmly presses on the van's brakes, bringing it to a halt. He turns off the engine and replies, "It's true. The farm is starting to show signs of wear and tear, but considering the employees we support, we simply don't have enough money at the moment to initiate repairs. For now, we have to make do with what we have."

Manav carefully reflects upon Neel's comment, giving them significant consideration. "I can see what I have and use it to pay for the equipment and renovations this farm needs to continue to operate," Manav offers. "It will give me a chance to contribute to what my family has created, and it's the least I can do."

"Don't feel pressured to do that," Neel tells Manav firmly. "The fact that you were able to come here and meet everyone means a lot already."

"You are giving me too much credit for nothing," Manav responds, nodding.

Neel restarts the car, and he and Manav drive back to the house. On their way there, Neel points out of his window to his left to show Manav the largest barn on the land. "Arvin built that by himself when he was just a teenager. You can climb a ladder on the side that'll lead you to the rooftop. From there, you get a view of the skies, and Arvin liked to watch the moon come out at night and sunrise in the morning, which is why he called it the First of Light Barn. There is also a small table and television inside, so you can spend some time there when you can."

As Manav glances at the infrastructure, he can't help but feel a sense of awe and admiration. He is particularly impressed by the level of coordination and planning that must have been required to build and maintain such a vast infrastructure.

He and Neel resume their drive and arrive back at the house, where Manav gets changed into different clothes, and for the remainder of the day, he helps the workers with their tasks. In the heat, he assists with planting seeds, harvesting crops, and ensuring the animals are well cared for by providing them with food and water. He also learns to operate heavy machinery, such as plows and tractors, to help manage the farm.

After working a long shift, everyone walks back home to relax for the evening, and Neel takes Manav for a tour around the house. It consists of four floors that are filled with bedrooms and washrooms and a large kitchen on the main floor.

"Our home is the residence for many of our workers until they're able to establish a life of their own," Neel explains as they walk through the home.

"Arvin stood for something bigger than himself, and I am stunned by everything I've seen today," Manav replies.

After Neel gives him a comprehensive tour of the house, Manav goes into his bedroom to do his nightly routine. After this, he grabs his phone from his charger and coat from his closet and leaves the house to visit the First of Light Barn to catch a glimpse of the night skies. He walks along the trail to the barn and sees many of the animals sleeping on the vibrant green grass in different areas of the farm.

He enters the section where the First of Light Barn is located, and as he is about to walk to the back to take the ladder to the rooftop, a medium-sized cow bumps him on his side. Manav turns and gently pets the animal. "You are not Cooper, but the next best thing."

He continues to the back of the barn, finds the ladder, and climbs it to the rooftop. Once he is there, he stands high and does a slow three-hundred-and-sixty-degree turn to see the entire farm, and then he lays down to watch the stars and moon. He unhooks the chain from around his neck and grips it firmly by the disc plate attached to it.

"Arvin, I don't know how you were able to accomplish what you did at a young age," Manav says as he gazes at the skies. "You must have had the weight of the world on your shoulders as you were looking out for so many people."

After reflecting for an extended period, Manav reaches into his pocket and takes out his phone to video call Anaya. The camera is pointed to the sky.

"Now that's a scene anyone would enjoy seeing," she says by way of greeting.

He flips the camera view to himself. "The community here is like nothing you have ever seen. It has been an eye-opening experience so far to watch everyone working together to care for this farm. Also, I talked to Maraino recently, and I'm taking his advice on changing my outlook on things. Being here has definitely changed my perspective."

Manav continues his conversation with Anaya as he makes his way back down from the rooftop to go back home. Once he reaches the bottom of the ladder, he sees the same cow that bumped into him earlier and points his camera at it to show Anaya. "I can't wait to come back home, and when I do, I might bring him with me."

"It will be exciting when you get back, but you are out of your mind if you bring him home," she says as she laughs.

He ends his conversation with her shortly after. Before he leaves, he takes one last look at the barn by doing a full lap around it. He runs his hand along the aged wood, observes the worn-out windows, and feels the creaking doors, and he can't help but notice the barn's outdated condition.

"I've got an idea to fix this," he whispers to himself.

Chapter Twenty-One

"I want you to know that your hard work here doesn't go unnoticed, day after day, Manav. Your contributions are truly valued," Neel says, his voice kind and appreciative.

During Manav's stay at his family's farm, he spends long hours helping the farm labourers with their tasks. Although he commits roughly ten to twelve hours each day supporting everyone, he doesn't feel physically exhausted because the feeling he gets from helping everyone motivates him. However, from his experience thus far, he has become more aware of how most of the farming equipment often stops operating and the lumber used for constructing their barns and farmhouses show signs of constant deterioration.

One afternoon, while working on the farm, he witnesses one of the tires on their tractor blow out, so he decides to take this issue into his own hands by driving into town to look for support. He arrives at a store called the Farming Services Shop, which offers farming equipment and skilled labour for renovation projects. Before going inside the store, he pauses to check the funds in his account to get a better idea of his spending limits. After viewing his savings, he locks his phone, greets an elderly employee that is sweeping the front of the shop, then proceeds to walk through the front doors.

He approaches the clerk standing at the store's front counter, giving him a straight, firm look. "My name is Manav," he starts, "and to be direct with you, my family's farm is in need of new equipment and renovations. I am wondering what services you can provide to help with this."

"Akash is my name," the clerk replies. "What do you specifically need?"

"Where should I begin? We have equipment that continues to break down, and much of our buildings, especially the house for our employees, are in desperate need of repairs," Manav says.

Following a brief conversation, Akash gains an understanding of Manav's needs, and then he takes out a fillable receipt that is organized by the names of the different equipment and services and begins to calculate the costs of Manav's request. Akash puts down his pen after a few minutes of writing and looks carefully over the bill himself. He then shows it to Manav.

Manav's eyes widen after viewing his estimate. "You want over thirty thousand dollars?" Manav shouts to him.

"And not a penny less than that," Akash replies calmly.

Manav stares at the steep price on the bill, then he crumples it and throws it onto the floor next to him. He puts both hands on the counter and tells him firmly, "This price is way too steep. Let's make a fair deal that will work for the both of us."

"Oh, you want me to cut you a deal?" Akash says, laughing. "How about you stop wasting my time? We have many people demanding our services, so we are not desperate to strike a deal with you. I suggest you leave the store now if you're not happy with our pricing."

Manav locks eyes with Akash, slowly steps away from the counter, and then walks out of the shop. He stands just outside the front entrance and observes people walking along the sidewalk. He sees someone smoking a cigarette, approaches them, and gives them a five-dollar bill and says, "I just need one."

This man hands Manav a cigarette, then lends him a lighter. Once he ignites his cigarette, he gives the lighter back and sits on the edge of the curb a few feet in front of the Farming Services Shop. As he smokes, he takes off his necklace and stares at the image engraved on the disc plate, then he gently places it flat on the ground beside him and looks straight at the road.

"Is there any chance you could spare some change?" a homeless person walking along the sidewalk with his empty grocery cart asks Manav.

Manav reaches into his pocket, hands him a ten-dollar bill, and says, "That's all I can give right now, but hopefully you can buy yourself a meal with that." Manav takes a puff of his cigarette as the man looks carefully at the money given to him. "We always have work available on our farm, too, so if you need extra money to make it out of your situation, working there will give you that opportunity."

Manav watches as the man takes a crumpled piece of paper and a pen from his pocket, ready to jot down the address. Once Manav gives him the complete address, the man folds the paper carefully and tucks it back into his pocket, and then he pushes his empty grocery cart to carry on with his day. The elderly store clerk, still sweeping the front entrance of the shop, watches this entire scene and approaches Manav with a curious gaze. Manav, feeling the weight of the clerk's stare, turns and looks back at him awkwardly, and then he focuses his attention on the road in front of him.

The clerk uses his broom to bring Manav's chain closer to him. He uses his brush to sweep at the disc plate, and his eyes widen and his jaw slightly drops when he sees the engraved image. He drops his broom to his side, grips Manav by his T-shirt, and attempts to lift him from his sitting position.

Manav shoves his arm away to defend himself, then he throws his cigarette to the ground and stands to confront the store clerk. The clerk rushes into the shop while Manav stares in disbelief, kneeling to grab his chain and fasten it around his neck. He watches the entrance of the shop, wondering what just happened.

The elderly store clerk returns outside with Akash.

Akash pauses and stares at Manav, then walks to him and puts his palm under his chain to take a closer look at it. "Arvin…he was a good man," he says to Manav. "This man here is my father, and before buying this shop, he had his own hurdles that he had to overcome as he was struggling with money and was always unsure where his next meal would come from. That was the case until he met Arvin. He provided my dad with work, food, and shelter, which changed his life. I'm surprised Arvin didn't reach out to us when he was alive about the current state of the farm, but then again, he was not the type to ask for any favours."

Akash walks to the front door of his store and flips the

Open sign to *Closed*. He looks back at Manav and tells him, "Let's get to work."

They walk to the back of the shop, where they and several other workers begin filling semi-trucks with equipment that the farm needs. Once they finish loading several types of machinery, tools, and lumber, Manav walks into the shop, takes off his chain, and places it in an empty envelope on the counter. He writes an address on it and puts it in the mailbox just outside the front door. Manav then walks to the back of the store again and takes a seat in one of the semi-trucks, and they all leave for Arvin's farm.

They drive for several minutes and eventually reach the long, narrow road that leads to the farm. The workers out on the fields pause to watch the semi-trucks carrying the equipment. The trucks come to a stop, and workers quickly rush toward them as they try to understand what is transpiring.

Manav slowly steps out of the truck, stares at everyone confidently, and shouts, "Let's turn this place around!"

The labourers respond positively to Manav's words, cheering him on and showing their appreciation for his efforts. Manav, along with Akash and the shop and farm workers, then begin unloading equipment from trucks and start the process of renovating the farm.

They replace the tractors, seed drills, and combine harvesters with newer models. They assist in improving the quality of the soil by bettering their drainage system and expanding the crop fields. With the lumber they receive, they construct new barns and farmhouses and renovate their older structures, including the First of Light Barn and the home where many of their employees reside.

While everyone continues to put in great effort to make

these upgrades, Manav steps away from his work to observe the drastic changes that have been made to Arvin's farm.

"These changes are going to go a long way for all the people here. How were you able to put this together?" Neel asks as he comes and stands next to him.

"It was not as challenging as you think it might've been. The workers at the shop knew Arvin, which motivated them to give the help they gave today," Manav replies.

They watch the workers for several minutes, then Neel reaches into his pocket and takes out an old photo that he hands to Manav. "I was cleaning out the house earlier and found this picture of Arvin holding you when you were just a few years old. He used to talk about you, and he said there was something special about you, and I would say I agree with him."

Manav glances at the photo carefully. "I'm only here for a limited time, so I'm doing what I can to help."

Chapter Twenty-Two

"We were able to come together today to improve this land," Akash says to Manav, "but with it getting dark out, we'll continue our work tomorrow."

"Your efforts today are going to make a change that will last for many years to come," Manav replies as he shakes Akash's hand.

Akash and his workers get into their trucks and drive away from the scene after spending the entire day supporting Manav in repairing his farm.

With sweat and dirt all over his clothes, Manav walks into the house, where he does his nighttime routine and meets the workers in the dining room for dinner. They continue to express their gratitude for the upgrades and renovations, and he is fulfilled by their compliments. After eating dinner with them, he goes upstairs to grab his coat and phone, then, as he has during his late evenings, he walks over to the First of Light Barn and climbs to the rooftop to get a good view of the farm and night skies.

He stands tall on the rooftop and scans the area as he is amazed by the renovations made to the farm, then he video calls his dad to show him these changes.

"It turned out better than expected," Manav's dad shares with him once he answers his call.

Manav takes a seat on the roof. "We were burning in the heat today, but everyone worked through it. We have much more that needs to be done tomorrow, especially with rebuilding some of the infrastructures."

"You did what you needed to do, and your mom and I can't wait to have you back here soon," his dad says with a warm smile. Manav nods in response, and his dad adds, "Hey, I noticed you're not wearing your chain. Did you leave it back at the house?"

"I mailed it out today," Manav replies calmly. "I think it's going to someone that represents what Arvin did."

They end their conversation shortly after, then Manav puts his phone at his side and lies down to see the dark sky and the bright stars. He glances at it and admires it while feeling fulfilled by what he accomplished today.

While lost in thought, from the corner of his eye, Manav sees a small, bright orange light coming from near the front gate of the farm. He stands to his feet to get a better look and sees a cloud of gray smoke emanating from there. He soon recognizes that what he is observing is a fire that is spreading quickly. He does not know how these flames ignited, but he understands that he needs to take action to prevent damage to Arvin's farm. Therefore, Manav quickly gets down from the rooftop, runs inside the barn to grab a fire extinguisher, and takes the motorcycle that is parked a few feet away from him to the fire. As he drives there, he notices that many of the farm animals are scattering as they are unsettled by the smoke in the air.

With his adrenaline pumping, Manav speeds to the front of the farm, where he meets raging fire threatening to consume everything in its path. Undeterred, Manav jumps into action and uses the fire extinguisher in his right hand to douse the powerful flames. After getting the fire under control, he takes a deep breath, scanning the area for any signs of the culprits responsible for the fire.

"Who's out there? Show yourself!" Manav shouts.

His eyes dart from one end of the property to the other, searching for any clues that might lead him to the perpetrators. Unexpectedly, a tall man creeps behind him and hits him with vicious punches.

Manav loses his grip on the fire extinguisher due to the attack. He instinctively backpedals to create space collect himself, and once he is able to steady his stance, he throws a single, line-drive punch that connects with the man's jaw.

This person collapses to the ground, unconscious, and Manav confidently approaches him. He grips him by the shirt and lifts him slightly from the ground to get a closer look at his physical characteristics, but he lets go of him as he does not recognize him.

When he turns around, he sees fires being ignited by two other men on the other side of the farm near the new machinery and buildings. Without hesitation, Manav sprints to his motorcycle and speeds toward them.

He first approaches the man pouring gasoline on one of

their new tractors. He parks his motorcycle near them, steps off of it, and confidently walks toward them. "You've got no idea who you are dealing with," Manav says in a commanding tone.

He grips the man by his shirt and pins him against the tractor, then, with every muscle in his body, he tosses him with full force to the ground.

Manav then shifts his focus to the third person, and his eyes widen when he recognizes they are standing next to First of Light Barn, attempting to spark a fire around its structure. He picks up a plank of wood lying next to him that is set ablaze that he will use to fight off this person. Despite the wood burning through his hand, his anger and courage because of this individual damaging this particular structure gives him the strength to keep fighting.

Manav walks towards the man with purposeful strides. With swift precision, he delivers two powerful strikes to the man's hip using the fiery piece of lumber. The impact is forceful, causing the man to collapse to the ground with a resounding thud. Though in pain, he remains conscious, his face contorted with agony. Manav walks to his side and leans into him. "Who are you? What are you doing here?" he shouts. He grips the man's chin and moves their head side to side to get a closer look, but, again, he does not recognize him.

As Manav continues to glance at this person as they lie in defeat, his eyes widen as he feels a cold, sharp object pressing into the middle of his back. He pivots to see someone pointing a gun at him.

"Arjin, how did you find me here?" Manav says in a slow, hesitant tone.

"Get inside the barn, and we'll talk in there," Arjin calmly replies. Arjin and the young man with tattoos that Manav struck with the piece of wood escort him inside the barn.

Arjin instructs Manav to take a seat in the chair that is beneath the harsh glare of a small ceiling light, and he has no choice but to comply. The young man with tattoos grabs the firearm from Arjin's hand and stands next to Manav with the weapon pointed directly at him.

Arjin takes a few steps toward him. "Manav, we looked out for you like a brother, and in return, you decided to turn on us like a coward. We asked you to bring out the bag we gave you at the Cavstros Hotel so we could sort our deal with Johnny, but you decided to run away from the scene. Many people were criminally charged, and our reputation was damaged."

Arjin pauses, his tone becoming more heated. "And on top of that, you had the nerve to talk down to me on the phone after you got out of prison. So, getting even with you was the only way to go. And just so you know, if I didn't find you, Johnny or Manny would've, because they were wanting payback, too."

Manav is left speechless, struggling to comprehend the truth that Arjin has been after him all along. He stares blankly at the floor before gaining the courage to look up at Arjin. "I just need to use my phone."

"To call for help? Not a chance," Arjin tells Manav firmly.

"I just need it for a little bit of time, Arjin. You have my word. I won't do anything suspicious," Manav pleads.

Arjin glances at the young man, giving a nod of approval, then turns his attention back to Manav. "Alright, you've got a few minutes, but that's it." Arjin then looks the young man and says, "Watch over him to make sure he does not try anything sneaky."

Manav looks at Arjin and the young man, then reaches into his pocket to take out his phone. First, he sends money transfer to

Noah and sends a text: *This is the money from poker night. This should cover your lawyer fees and everything in between. You have a clean slate now, brother.*

Noah immediately replies to his message: *You only needed to send me twenty bucks, not the thousands you just sent.*

Manav then contacts his dad and says: *I understand now. You just wanted me to do good for myself by wanting me to make smart choices.*

Finally, he reaches out to Anaya and tells her: *Someone that sticks by you through thick and thin.*

He then locks his phone and drops it to the ground in front of him.

Arjin smirks at Manav, then walks to the front doors of the barn and forcefully opens them to show Manav that the two men he attacked earlier are setting large fires across the farm. The vicious flames they have created are dismantling the machinery and buildings.

"Let's handle our business so I don't get caught in this fire too!" Arjin shouts. He closes the doors and walks back to Manav.

Manav remains surprised by what he is witnessing and engages in his deep thoughts. "None of this matters, none of this at all," he tells Arjin. "All my life. My entire life, I've always felt like I was not good enough, and it was challenging to overcome this feeling as I struggled with it daily. I just hope my story will be told to the next person to inspire them to make better choices than I did."

Manav turns his head slightly to his left, where he sees a staticky, gray television playing sports highlights.

"This is a video of the world's greatest basketball player breaking the all-time scoring record with his fadeaway jump shot!" the sports host enthusiastically shouts. "He continues to build on his reputation of being the best." The host then transitions to another segment about an athlete receiving insurmountable support to be released from prison after being convicted.

"I just hope my story will be told," Manav repeats as he smiles at the television. "But then again, maybe it will vanish over time, considering I am just an average citizen."

Arjin steps closer to Manav. "You aren't moving anyone with your speech, so you can keep quiet."

Despite Arjin's hateful comment, Manav continues to express his thoughts to him. "I've realized from my experiences that the insecurity I tried to fulfill in the short term wasn't worth the complications I faced in the long term, and after having multiple experiences that could have cost me my life, I now recognize that none of this matters. The materialism and money fade over time, but the way I can inspire the world, just like those I impacted at this farm, will live forever. But, having said that, this is all difficult to achieve as we are bombarded with messages that continue to tell us that we are not good enough the way we are. All of this oddly makes you wonder what the meaning of strength is. Is it as simple as displaying a tough, artificial persona, or can it be one's ability to persevere through challenging tasks that will positively impact others?"

After a deep breath, Manav adds, "When I was with you, Arjin, whether I was sitting next to you in your car or spent time with you at your place, I only saw a person that was confused about themselves. So I have to say, what were you missing? Did you feel like you needed to prove yourself? Did you have trouble connecting with others? What were you missing? Did people close to you have trouble standing up to you when you were acting out of hand? Or did you have a tough environment that caused you to act out? Whatever it may be, all I know is that every time I saw you, I saw a bit of me, and now, the second chapter for myself will never be written."

Manav's comments catch Arjin off guard, then he looks at the young man with the firearm and says, "Enough is enough. It's time to get out of here."

The young man presses the trigger.

Manav's breath immediately becomes lighter as it begins to fade. As he slowly weakens after each second passes, the doors of the barn burst open, and through the shadow of the flames, Manav sees dozens of farm workers rushing into the barn and viciously attacking Arjin and his peer. He is inspired to see that the farm workers came to support him, but he slowly loses his vision of this scene as a white light overtakes him. He then sees nothing but a set of bright stairs that he begins to climb, and as Manav takes each step, he sees many significant events from his life play out and becomes completely in-tuned with his thoughts and actions.

I move up the staircase, and as I look to my left, I see images of myself playing at the park with my mom and dad when I was five years old. I appreciate those moments with them. I take a few more steps and look to my right, where I see images of the first time I met Devin when I was just seven years of age. His dad was helping my family purchase a home, and we have been friends ever since, as he always looked out for me.

I continue to move up the staircase while looking side-to-side, and I surprisingly see Jairaj playing outdoor hockey with his older brother. He has a large smile and not his typical angry look. There must be a deeper story to him that I never understood.

Another image appears from when I gave change to a random stranger at the bus stop, and I hope that helped you at that moment. I see a time when I appeared upset while looking out my window as my dad left for work. I did not understand why he was working long hours from week to week, but I should have been more understanding about our financial situation.

I see moments of myself celebrating some of my biggest wins in basketball and soccer with my teammates. I come across images of me hugging Maraino. He is a true supporter that I look up to.

As I reach the top of the staircase, I see Cooper and give him one last pet on his back. I look up and see Arvin, and I immediately tell him how inspired I am by how he used his farm to support many people. He walks with me further down the clouds, where the air becomes fresher and cleaner. Big man, I see you. He looks back and replies, "What's up, what's up?" then takes a dribble and continues to work on that skyhook shot. Arvin then places one hand on my shoulder and tells me it's time to go back.

The bright light that Manav is experiencing reaches its peak.

Chapter Twenty-Three

Several years later...

"We've made it to our stop! Feel free to grab your things and go about your day," the bus driver calls out cheerfully to everyone.

Jay and Ryan stare at the driver, then they gather their belongings and step off the bus.

"First semester of many to go," Ryan says to Jay. They look up at the imposing red brick building that serves as the university's home. Ryan adds, "We might as well get used to this place because who knows how many years we'll be here?"

Jay nods at Ryan. "We should make our way to the gym to see that presentation our professor wanted us to see before class, but it sounds like it could be a long and boring day if we have to go to that."

Jay stops by the newspaper stand for the daily paper, then he and Ryan walk to the convenience store to buy some snacks and drinks to prepare for their school day.

"This should keep me awake for the day," Jay tells Ryan as he takes his first sip of coffee. They start walking to the gymnasium, and Jay reads newspapers along the way. He turns to Ryan and says, "Have you seen the news today? It says a man recently woke up from a coma after sustaining life-threatening injuries years ago."

"I heard about that case," Ryan replies. "I heard a coma can be a long dream that'll tell you a unique story like nothing you have ever experienced."

Jay keeps his attention to the newspaper while he and Ryan walk through the campus. They reach the gymnasium, and they see that several hundred people have gathered for the event, creating an atmosphere of anticipation and excitement. The lights begin to dim, indicating this event is starting soon. Jay and Ryan weave through the traffic of people and secure a spot near the back next to the emergency exit.

As they wait, a tall presenter wearing a black and blue suit and a gold chain with the First of Light Barn engraved on the disc plate walks onto the stage.

"Hey, everyone, I hope you're having a great day so far," the man says to the large crowd. "My name is Professor Devin Gill, and I am putting on this presentation for you all this morning."

Professor Gill talks for a few hours about different topics, such as the media and its influences, being an independent thinker, and the importance of strong coping strategies. He shares insightful information that captivates the crowd, and once the presentation concludes, Jay and Ryan gather their belongings and finish the rest of their day at school.

Ryan offers Jay a ride home after class, and upon arriving, he turns to Jay with a smirk. "Partying and textbooks, man. This university thing is going to be easy," he says confidently.

Jay nods back at him. "It's a little bit of both, but more textbooks and less partying. Surprisingly, I actually learned a lot today."

They shake hands and exchange their farewells.

Jay walks to the front of his house, and before he opens his door, he sees his neighbour, Mase, and his friends smoking cigarettes and drinking alcohol in front of Mase's home.

"Jay!" Mase shouts to him, a teasing tone in his voice. "It must have been another boring day at school. Besides sitting at your desk, studying and sweating, what else is there to it?" Jay turns and glances at him, then Mase adds, "Come here and let's talk for a second."

Jay hesitates but eventually sets his backpack down and approaches the small group. He shakes all of their hands in greeting.

Mase tells him with a slight rasp as he continues to puff on his cigarette, "You should quit wasting your time studying. You don't even know if that'll pay off, plus nobody cares about it."

"Just leave him alone," Mase's girlfriend says, sitting on the porch as she looks at her social media page on her phone. "He's doesn't understand what matters and has always been a weird kid."

Mase glances at his girlfriend, then refocuses his attention on Jay. "Regardless of his choices, I have a good idea. Behind you, just watch that old lady for a moment."

Jay turns around and sees an elderly lady getting into her car, a gray-coloured Mercedes Benz S-Class. She starts the engine and sits in the driver's seat for a few minutes, then steps out of her car in a frenzy and quickly paces inside her home.

"Poor lady must be at least over seventy years old, and she does this same routine every time," Mase tells him. "Whenever she leaves her house and enters her car, she runs back inside her home thinking she forgot something important while leaving her car on and doors unlocked. All she is really doing is making her purse that she left in her car an easy grab. What do you think, Jay? She probably keeps at least a few thousand dollars with her, considering the car she drives."

"She definitely seems up there in age with how fragile she looked when walking in her home," Jay replies.

Jay then turns and stares at Mase, and Mase and his peers give a confident but also intimidating look to Jay.

"I say we all get paid today, including you," Mase says, putting out his cigarette. "It's an easy grab. All you got to do is walk over to that car and get her purse. We will keep an eye out from here. If she steps out of her house, then we'll give you a signal to run."

"Sounds easy enough," Jay admits. "But to be honest, a few dollars isn't really worth your praise. I think I'll pass. You're right about one thing, though. Diving into all those books can get pretty dull, and who knows how the next few years will unfold."

Mase opens his mouth to speak, but Jay doesn't give him a chance. "But I'd rather be recognized for something more positive than valued by you for robbing an old lady. I don't expect you to understand, but I will choose the way my chapter is written."

Afterword

Dear readers,

I express my heartfelt thanks to each and every one of you who has purchased a copy of my book. Your decision to embrace my work and embark on this literary journey with me is a gift beyond measure.

With deepest gratitude,

Rahul Minhas

About the Author

Rahul Minhas is an educator and community support worker. He was born and raised in Surrey, BC. His passion for supporting others led him to pursue a master's program in counselling, which he is currently completing. Rahul's diverse experience in education and community support has allowed him to make a meaningful impact on the lives of those he works with. Through his unwavering commitment to his profession, Rahul has proven himself to be a compassionate and dedicated advocate for the well-being of others.

Manufactured by Amazon.ca
Bolton, ON

35001357R00094